Stardust
Baby

Stardust Baby

Lisa Lawlor

mB

MIRROR BOOKS

First published by Mirror Books in 2021

Mirror Books is part of Reach plc
10 Lower Thames Street
London EC3R 6EN

www.mirrorbooks.co.uk

Print ISBN 978-1-913406-45-5
eBook ISBN 978-1-913406-44-8

Typeset by Danny Lyle

Printed and bound in Great Britain by
CPI Group (UK) Ltd, Croydon, CR0 4YY

A CIP catalogue record for this book is available from the British Library.

3 5 7 9 10 8 6 4 2

In memory of my parents,
Francis and Maureen.

Contents

In the early morning of February 14th, 1981, 48 young people died in a fire at the Stardust disco in north Dublin. This notorious tragedy is known in Ireland as the Stardust disaster. At the time of writing, the survivors and the victims' families are continuing to fight for justice.

Foreword

You couldn't but notice Lisa Lawlor at that press conference in a Dublin hotel, on a Thursday morning 26th September 2019.

Among the elderly men and women – most of them parents who had lost children in the Stardust inferno 38 years previously – was this striking young woman.

The families were there to hear Lynn Boylan, then a former Sinn Fein MEP, announce that inquests into the 48 deaths would be re-opened.

I had covered the Stardust families' campaign for justice since my earliest days in journalism, but had not met Lisa before. She was 40, she told me. She had been orphaned by the tragedy, and was known for most of her childhood as the "Stardust Baby".

The 1981 Stardust disaster had affected her whole life.

She was 17 months old when her father, Francis (25), and mother, Maureen (23) went out "for a few drinks on Valentine's night".

"I have no memories whatsoever of my two parents other than the pain, loss and complete and utter devastation," she told me. "I grew up in the shadow of this disaster. I lived with my father's parents. I'm an only child and the Stardust left me on my own in this world. My grandmother was crying day in, day out."

"I remember starting school and kicking the legs off the teacher because I just did not want to be there, or anywhere. I knew there was something wrong but I didn't know what it was. Part of me died and I was never normal, whatever that is. My heart was broke."

She told me how it had affected "every relationship", how it had been "the loss that's always there. It's been very tough, very lonely. It's tough being me.

"My grandparents died in 2000 and 2003 and there were times I felt 'I'm done' and 'I can't go on'. Life was just too hard to cope with… I have a wound that just won't heal."

As we approach its 40th anniversary, Stardust remains one of Ireland's most shameful wounds. That 48 young people died needlessly is horrendous. The failure of the State to make any real attempt to uncover why they died is reprehensible.

Through decades it has been solely down to the doggedness of grieving families, who would not be silenced, that each, seemingly small, new piece of evidence emerged, cumulatively tearing apart the State's account.

It was not arson, as the Charles Haughey-appointed Keane Tribunal would have had us believe in 1981. The fire did not start on a seat in the venue's West Alcove, as was suggested from the outset. There was a witness, Brenda Kelly, who saw the fire start in the roof-space who has never been asked for her account, by any statutory investigation.

One cannot help but wonder whether the litany of failures was deliberate, or negligent. Or whether the young, working-class lives were somehow expendable to those who both then and now control the narrative.

Some months after I first met Lisa, she called me to say she planned to write a book about how the Stardust tragedy impacted her life. As she sets out her story and her unanswered questions here, the very least the Irish State owes her and all the Stardust families, is the truth.

Kitty Holland

Prologue

Stardust Baby

I know that my parents loved me.

"You were the light of their life," my family told me. "They were totally smitten with their baby girl. The only wonder is that they went out at all that night; they never liked to leave you. Your mammy just danced attendance on you all the time, as if you were the most perfect baby in the world."

I was just a little tot, aged a year and a half, when my parents died, but I have heard so much about them and that awful night, that sometimes it feels as though I had been there myself; as though I saw the fire, smelled its fumes, and heard it crackle as it destroyed the Stardust and all those young lives.

My aunts and other members of the family told me endless stories about them – Maureen and Francis – and I have been able to piece together much of what happened on the last night of their young lives, that cold February night and early morning. I will never know all the details, and no one ever will, but from everything that I have heard, it went like this:

"We've hardly been out since the wedding," Francis said, "and even less since Lisa was born. What harm could it do? It's Valentine's weekend; we should take some time to ourselves for once."

"I don't know… I don't think it's a great idea."

Maureen was not sure at all about going out. She was always very protective of me, even though I was 17 months now, and growing into a toddler. I was her first child, and she doted on me because she had had several miscarriages before I came along, and then a difficult time giving birth, as the result of a bad break she had suffered in a traffic accident as a teenager.

Maureen, my mother, hated leaving me alone, and kept me spotlessly clean and always dressed in beautiful clothes from good shops like Byer's and Switzer's, which were two upmarket department stores that only sold the best. She hardly even let my aunties and cousins touch me, and inadvertently hurt the feelings of my father's family more than once by asking them if they had washed their hands before picking me up. Now, she hated the thought of leaving me with a babysitter, especially because I was still getting over a cough, and she had been spending all her time indoors with me, waiting for me to get better. She was also pretty sure that she was pregnant again – and had even told a few friends that she was – even though it was far too early for her to be showing and, given her medical history, she did not know whether or not the pregnancy would last.

"Go on, it'll be Valentine's Day at midnight..." Francis said persuasively. "There's a disco on in the Stardust. I'm after gettin' an invitation to go from Paddy Rafferty. It's going to be great. There's going to be a dance competition; it'll be fun."

Disco dancing was still big at the time, and a lot of the young people from north Dublin entered contests at the Stardust, vying to be the best dancer in the nightclub and go home with a trophy. There was a prize for the best boy, and for the best girl.

"We'll be the oldest people there!" Maureen grumbled.

Francis just laughed: "Will you go on outta that," he said. "We're still young and gorgeous!"

"*And* it's Friday the 13th," Maureen said. "It's supposed to be bad luck to do anything on Friday the 13th."

But Maureen had started to smile. Francis had won her over, like he always did.

"Now you're just being daft," said Francis, lovingly. "You go and put on something pretty. You know I like to show off my beautiful wife."

The Stardust in Artane, opposite the Artane Castle Shopping Centre, was the trendiest venue in north Dublin and all the young people flocked there to dance and strut their stuff to the latest tunes by groups like Madness, Queen and Spandau Ballet. The club was huge, with two bars, a dance floor, a stage, and areas for seating. Maureen, despite her misgivings, was tempted by the prospect of a night out. She had had her pretty blonde hair blow-dried and sprayed and she had a lovely new outfit ready to go. Since becoming a mother, she had taken very little time off, and she had such high standards for how the house was kept that she was always busy. She did not often get the chance to just relax and be young the way she had before the baby was born.

"It won't do Lisa any harm to stay with the babysitter for once," Francis said. "She'll be fast asleep soon and her cough is nearly gone. She won't even know that we're not there, and when she wakes up in the morning, we can take her into our bed for a cuddle."

Maureen started to relent: "Okay then. I suppose it can't do any harm. We don't need to stay out late."

"'Course we don't. We can just go for a little while and then come straight back home to the babba. We're not old yet, love. We're still allowed to have a bit of fun. There's no harm in it. There'll be plenty of time to relax in front of the telly when we're older."

Francis took his wedding ring off and put it on top of the telly before they went out, to keep it safe.

There were 846 young people crammed into the disco that cold night, all dressed up, excited, and having a great time. The scents of Brut cologne and Charlie perfume filled the air. Maureen and Francis had planned to come home earlier to let the babysitter off, but they were having so much fun that they stayed on later than they had originally intended; they did not want to miss the dance competition, which was still in full swing at one in the morning.

At about half past one, a girl sitting in the area known to management as the West Alcove noticed that it was suddenly getting very hot, and she assumed that the heating had just been turned on.

The dance competition came to an end and the winners – a girl and a boy – were awarded with their trophies while the crowd stamped, cheered, and held up their pint glasses in celebration.

A few people noticed smoke, and then flames, in an unoccupied area of the nightclub, but the management and staff still had no idea that something was wrong. The DJ put on some more tunes, and everyone headed back onto the dancefloor.

Minutes later, more people started becoming aware of the flames beginning to lick the backs of the chairs in the area where they were sitting. The management was alerted to the situation, and after a few minutes the music stopped.

"There's no reason to panic," the DJ said over the speaker system. "There's a small fire on the premises, nothing to worry about, and we're going to ask you all to evacuate in an orderly fashion and to stay outside until it has been taken care of. Hopefully, you can come back in soon."

Staff members carried fire extinguishers to the area where seats were beginning to burn, thinking that they could extinguish the flames quickly and easily. Laughing and joking, people started to amble slowly towards the exit, assuming that they would go outside for a few minutes and then be allowed back in again. The lights then went out, but the staff emerged with lit candles, and continued to reassure everyone that it was all going to be just fine.

All the young people had been drinking and having a good time, and the mood remained high. There were jokes and a bit of jostling as they continued to move towards the exits, some of them still holding their pints and their Babychams, bumping into one another and swearing light-heartedly when their drinks spilled.

At 1:42 in the morning, a young man called Peter O'Toole used the only telephone on the premises to dial 999 to report the theft of his girlfriend's handbag to the guards. While he was making the report, he noticed the fire and it was recorded in the police transcript, as were the screams and cries of the dancers as they suddenly realised what was happening.

The true extent of the fire was more apparent from outside at first. A woman who lived about 200m away saw the flames several minutes before anyone inside was aware that something was wrong, and she called the fire brigade. A brigade was dispatched, but long before it could reach the discotheque, the flames – which had been burning for some time in the roof-space of the building, where cooking oils and other combustible items were stored – had burst through the flammable ceiling, which was now melting and dripping onto the young people below, setting the seating and carpets on fire as well as the disco patrons' clothing and lacquered hair. The lights went out, the dancehall filled with thick, black smoke and everyone panicked and started clambering over one another, screaming and roaring, desperately trying to escape. The fire was roaring too, audibly now – crackling loudly as it raced across the ceiling and through the furniture, destroying everything it encountered.

For many, the attempt to escape was fruitless, as several of the fire doors were padlocked, and the windows in the toilets had iron bars that made them impossible to escape through. The fire brigade tried but failed to remove the bars from outside, while the disco patrons who were stuck inside screamed and begged for help, grabbing at the bars even though they were too hot to touch and seared their flesh. Many had made it safely outside, but for the moment nobody knew who was still in the fire or what was happening to them.

As the authorities realised how serious the fire was, ambulances from all the hospitals in Dublin, and even the Airport Fire Rescue Service, were sent to the scene. Buses were also sent to take away the wounded, and the local pirate radio stations asked anyone in the area with a car to go to the club and see if they could help.

Many of the parents of the girls and boys at the disco had been staying up late, drinking tea and listening to the radio until the young ones came home and they knew that they were safe; they fled their houses when they heard the news and made their way to the chaotic scene in their cars and on foot, hoping against hope that it would not be as bad as it sounded and that their darling girls and boys would be all right.

It was pandemonium in the Stardust and in the grounds outside it. Those who were still alive were running over each other, trampling one another into the ground in their attempts to get to safety. Friends and couples got separated from one another and adrenaline and pure instinct took over as each person did their best to save themselves.

Francis – my dad – managed to get out of the inferno and into the cold night air. He took some deep breaths, which must have hurt his scorched lungs, and then he started to run around, looking for Maureen among the huddled groups of young people standing outside in a state of shock while the fire brigade did its best to keep the situation calm.

"Has anyone seen Maureen?" Francis asked the panic-stricken teenagers. "Where's my Maureen?"

None of them knew who Maureen was. They just shook their heads. Some of them were crying and unable to speak at all. Francis soon realised that Maureen was not there. She had not managed to get out. She was still inside.

"I'm going back in," Francis said. "I'm going to get her."

Francis filled his lungs with air and ran back into the fire. Nobody tried to stop him. Neither Francis nor Maureen ever came out again.

I have always wondered what my parents' last thoughts were and what happened in their final few minutes on earth. Did Dad reach Mum at all, or did he die without finding her? Did they realise that their lives were about to end? Did they try to comfort one another before it was too late? Did they suffer?

Did they think of me? I like to think that their baby girl was the last thing they thought about before they closed their eyes forever. But sometimes I allow myself to feel angry with my father for choosing my mother over me and, in the process, making me an orphan.

Back in our little house in Finglas – the house that was my mother's pride and joy, second only to me, because she kept it so spotless and beautiful – I was all alone. When the news came on the radio that evening that there was a terrible fire at the Stardust, the teenage girl who had been hired to mind me ran out of the house in a panic, because one of her family members was at the disco. In her fright, she must have completely forgotten about me, or maybe she assumed that someone else would come to take care of me in her absence. I was all alone until 11 the next morning, when my mother's parents, Paddy and Elizabeth Farrell, came to get me. By that stage, I was in a state of utter panic. My nappy was full, and I was standing in my cot and screaming, beating my little head against the bars as though I knew that something terrible had happened.

Just a couple of kilometres away, medical and recovery workers were still fishing through what was left of the Stardust for human remains. The recovered bodies were often still hot: so hot that they had to be hosed down before they could be loaded into an ambulance and brought to the morgue in the city centre. Many of those who had died had exploded in the intense heat, and human remains were scattered from one end of the venue to the other. Most of the men who were involved in this work were traumatised by what they had seen, but in Ireland in 1981 counselling was not on offer for them and nobody even suggested it. They had no choice but to work on and deal with the tears and the nightmares afterwards.

The newspapers were full of the fire for weeks. They could not get enough of it and the papers were flying off the shelves. Almost all the people who had died at the Stardust were teenagers, who should have had their whole lives ahead of them. The whole nation was in shock and mourning for the many young lives that had been so pointlessly lost. Masses were held, and every night on the news there was an update on the recovery of the bodies and the current condition of the wounded survivors.

Maureen and Francis – Mum and Dad – were among the oldest victims, and they were the only married couple who were parents, which made me the only Stardust orphan. 48 people in total, with an average age of 19 and a half, died in the fire,128 were admitted to hospital for treatment, and 86 were treated in out-patient units. Of the dead, eight died of multiple burns, eight died of traumatic shock resulting from their burns, and various other fire-related injuries were given as the official cause of death for the remaining victims.

Most of the dead were from the local area of Artane, a working-class neighbourhood, and for every person who died, whole families were left devastated. 22 families lost more than one loved one to the fire. For months afterwards, the area was like a ghost town as an entire community mourned.

Francis's body was identified and released to the family for burial first. Later, after a number of days, so was Maureen's, even though her remains were so badly damaged that there was no clear way to identify her for sure; the coroner relied on the fact that she had broken a hip as a young girl, although the heat of the fire had fractured the bones of many of the deceased. Nobody knows if Maureen really was pregnant when she died, as she had suspected: her remains were so charred, it was impossible to tell. The coroner's report relating to my mother ("number 31" of the victims) lays out starkly the terrible condition of her body and the difficulty they had in assigning a name to it. Coroner Robert Towers wrote that the body was so damaged that the head was almost completely destroyed, and it was impossible to take fingerprints, while no jewellery was found. She was barely recognisable as having once been a human being. He concluded that death had resulted from burns.

Even as they mourned, the Stardust families were put under huge pressure to arrange the burials as soon as possible, despite the fact that some bodies could only be identified by the jewellery they wore, while others could not be identified at all.

After the fire, the government seemed to be helping to smooth things over as quickly as they could. Rumours spread that the Butterly family, the owners of the nightclub, were very well-connected.

The Stardust funerals, largely funded by the Lord Mayor of Dublin's charity fund, went on for weeks as the bodies were identified. Public interest was so great that the gardaí often had to provide security. With each funeral, thousands of people lined the streets, and the city came to a standstill as the deceased were driven from the morgue in the city centre to their funeral Masses in the various churches on the Northside. The victims were so young, it was impossible not to be moved. Some of the Stardust victims could not be identified, and were buried in a mass grave. Of the others, many were given identifications that were dubious at best, as the remains were very badly damaged and DNA testing was in its infancy.

Francis and Maureen's funeral – a group funeral with a number of other victims – was held in Donnycarney church in Artane. The families were shellshocked, and the crowds were enormous; the church was packed to capacity, and mourners spilled outside into the church grounds. Many of the young people who had survived the fire managed to make it to the funeral to say goodbye to their friends; some of them still wore bandages on their wounds. People have told me about seeing me there, a little speck of a child just barely managing to stand on her own two feet, clutching her grandmother's hand. Although, obviously, I do not remember the funeral, I am glad that I was there.

The first inquiry into the fire was held later that year. Rumours were flying about how the fire had started and whose fault it was, and the official investigation (which had been ordered by Taoiseach Charlie Haughey, who had promised to do everything he could) did nothing to help.

The owners and management of the Stardust were heavily criticised for the fact that the emergency exits had been padlocked on the night of the fire, but the suggestion that someone inside the disco had deliberately lit the fire in an act of arson was held up. This effectively blamed the young people who lost their lives in the Stardust for their own deaths, and set the Butterly family up to receive a huge insurance pay-out.

At this point, no arrangements were made for compensation for the families of the victims and survivors, none of whom could afford the costs of bringing a legal case on their own: that would come later.

Anyone from Dublin knows that if the disco had been in an affluent Southside suburb, rather than a gritty working-class area of the Northside, nobody would have blamed the victims for their own deaths; that was adding insult to injury and everyone on the Northside knew it.

Somehow, despite breaking several laws with regard to fire safety regulations not only on the night of the fire, but also on other occasions previously identified by a safety inspector, the owners of the Stardust, the Butterly family, never apologised for the terrible events that took place on their watch, and never faced charges of any sort. On the contrary, they received substantial compensation for their claim for malicious damages from the state because of the initial finding that the fire was the result of arson. This was a finding that was later categorically disproved, but it prevented the survivors and their families from suing the nightclub's owners and management for corporate manslaughter or negligence.

The 600-page tribunal report, which was published in June 1982, outlines the background to the Stardust, the evidence collected from the disaster, and the conclusions reached by Judge Ronan Keane that were supposed to justify this outcome. The families involved were left to fight for justice on their own.

The Stardust disaster was a tragedy on a grand scale; the grief it caused for survivors or victims' family members has had a ripple effect throughout the years, and the generations, that followed.

Not a day has gone by since then that I have not thought about my parents, Maureen and Francis. They are with me when I wake up, and they are with me when I go to sleep. I have always asked my parents for help during the difficult periods of my life.

Maureen and Francis's young faces, never to grow older, look out at me from the only photograph I have of the three of us together. That photograph is precious to me: a tangible record of the brief relationship we had, and how I was loved by them. I treasure my father's wedding ring, left on the television before he went out that awful night. My grandmother wore it on a chain around her neck for years before giving it to me, and now I wear it on my finger every day. I will give it to whichever of my three children gets married first, as a way of keeping a little bit of my father alive, and of showing him that I will always love him.

An official report into the Stardust disaster warned that the children of affected families were likely to grow up experiencing mental health issues potentially as severe as those suffered by the survivors. I have lived with crippling anxiety all my life, and I have no doubt that the fire, its aftermath, and the impact it had on the emotional health of my family members, is the reason why.

I will always wonder what my life might have been like if things had been different – if Mum and Dad had not gone to the Stardust at all, or even if Dad had not run back into the flames to find Mum and had lived. If I had not had to grow up with the label "Stardust Baby".

All my life, the word "Stardust" has been whispered around me: a word so terrible that it cannot be proclaimed aloud, but must always be discussed in hushed tones. This was like a rot at the heart of my family, damaging relationships, tearing friendships apart, and pushing those who were already vulnerable for a variety of reasons towards a cliff-edge of self-destruction.

Many years after the fire, I am here to tell you that no good comes from secrets and obfuscation, and that we can only grow when we shed a light on even the darkest experiences in our lives. That is true for individuals like me, and it is also true for societies like Ireland.

Ireland has been working hard in recent years to uncover the truth about some of its darkest secrets, but the Stardust disaster and its aftermath is a story that has still not been completely told.

I cannot tell the story of other families, but I can share the story of mine.

People will say that I am superstitious, or that I am imagining things, but I honestly believe that – somehow – Mum and Dad are looking down on me and guiding me as I share our experiences, and that they want them to be known.

This is our account.

1

Francis and Maureen

Everything I know about my parents is from other people's stories. When I was a child, I was so hungry for information about my mum and dad that I would cling to whatever scraps about their lives I heard from anyone who mentioned them. Even now, I am always delighted to meet anyone who knew them, and to pick up a few titbits of information about what they were like. To this day, I examine my own face, and the faces of my children, for resemblances to Francis or Maureen, and I am happy when I think I find them.

Because I grew up with my father's parents, I know more about my dad and his childhood, but I have also been able to put together a picture of what my mother was like. So, please let me introduce to you Francis and Maureen Lawlor, two ordinary young Dubliners who became famous in the worst of all possible ways, when their young lives were extinguished by the most infamous fire in modern Irish history. We will start with Francis:

Francis, who was born on 3 September 1955, was the third eldest of 12 children. They were: Mary, Robert, Francis, Carol, Don, Denis, Gerard and Evelyne (who were twins), Martin, Edel, and Alison and Adrian (who were also twins). My grandmother, Lally, had also lost twins shortly after their birth, so she had 11 pregnancies altogether.

The Lawlor family lived in an old house on Seville Place, Sheriff Street, in Dublin's north inner city. When Francis was a little boy, the Sheriff Street area was inhabited by traditional "salt of the earth" families – working class people who worked hard, played hard, and fiercely loved their children, their city, and their faith.

My grandparents, Lally and Robin, were purebred Dubliners. She was born in a flat in Liberty House, one of Dublin's earlier council developments, and he was born in Talbot Street in the north inner city, which was both residential and commercial at that time. Lally used to tease Robin about his supposedly loftier origins: "He thinks he's great because he grew up in a house!" she always said.

The Sheriff Street area, where Lally and Robin settled as a young married couple, was like a snapshot of Dublin history, combining big old Georgian houses that had once been the rather grand homes of well-to-do merchants in the 18th century with badly-built council homes from the 1950s and everything in between. This mishmash of architecture is sandwiched between some of Dublin's most popular and prestigious shopping areas and the industrial landscape of the old canal area, today a shiny new financial district, but until recently a very run-down industrial spot blighted with dereliction and vacant sites.

The Lawlor family home – which Lally and Robin had bought for £700 before their first baby, Mary, was born in the early 1950s – was large and comfortable. It was one of a small terrace of Georgian houses with two big storeys over a basement, and a long garden out the back. It was furnished with antique furniture and the floral curtains, carpets and wallpaper that Lally liked. It was an ideal family home for such a big family. The house was large enough to have the tradition-al front room that was reserved for special occasions, such as when someone died or got married or the parish priest came to visit. That was where Lally kept all her treasures. She was very house-proud and always on the look-out for pretty things to put on display. The children hardly dared go inside because that room was always kept looking "nice" for honoured guests.

Lally loved being a mother and she was very good at it. She was loving, caring, and kind; her arms were always open for a hug and she adored babies – her own and anyone else's. She was a traditional housewife who took great pride in her work. The food in the house was always home-made, and she cooked all the traditional Dublin dishes: a rich Dublin coddle with sausages; bacon, cabbage, and potatoes; pressed pig's cheek or pig's tail; beef stew with home-made dumplings. Lally had so many children that, to make dinner, she needed to use a pot that was almost comically large: big enough to fit a child.

On Sundays there was a full roast dinner with two types of meat, two types of potatoes, gravy, and vegetables, followed by dessert, which might be sponge cake, coconut cake, or a range of the other home-made sweets that Lally loved to bake.

Lally was very particular about the quality of the ingredients she used to feed her children. Even though she could have bought everything locally, she swore by the butchers and greengrocers on Meath Street, a lively market street on the south side of the inner city, lined with traditional shops and the stalls of outdoor vendors. As Meath Street was some distance away, Lally had to get a lift to go and do her shopping there.

Robin had a good job as a plumber; his skills were highly regarded and he was never out of a job and made good money. He had worked on the plumbing in some of the most well-known buildings in Dublin. Robin worked very hard, and he also liked a drink – he always stopped for a pint (or sometimes a few pints) of Guinness on the way home.

Robin and Lally had a strong traditional marriage. He was the provider and she was the nurturer. They were each proud of what they did in their own sphere of influence, and they worked hard together to take care of their family. Like most Dublin families at that time, their faith was important to them. Lally made sure that everyone went to Mass and got their communion, and special days like First Holy Communions and Confirmations were celebrated in style for each and every child.

Lally was deeply devoted to the Dublin saint Matt Talbot (despite not yet being canonised, inner-city Dubliners nevertheless consider him a saint and take great pride in him being one of them). He was a holy man and ascetic who lived in the inner city, where he died in 1925. Initially interred in the Glasnevin suburb, since 1972 he has been buried in Our Lady of Lourdes Church in Séan McDermott Street, around the corner from Lally and Robin's home.

Lally prayed to Matt Talbot regularly, especially when someone she knew was struggling with a drink problem. She had a whole roster of saints to whom she prayed depending on the circumstances at hand: Saint Jude for lost causes; Saint Anthony for lost keys; Saint Teresa, the Little Flower, when somebody was ill. Lally could talk about these saints as though she knew them all personally and one had the impression that they were on first-name terms with each other.

All the Lawlor kids were taught to respect their faith and were reminded of it every day, because Lally had an altar in the corner of the living room for all her holy pictures and statues: the Sacred Heart of Jesus, whose eyes seemed to follow the children when they walked about; the Infant of Prague in his shiny red dress; the Blessed Virgin Mary, and a plastic bottle of holy water from Lourdes in the shape of the Virgin Mary with a lid in the form of a blue crown. Lally would open the holy water bottle and sprinkle it on someone who was about to go on a trip, or before exams; if someone was unwell, she encouraged them to take a sip of holy water to help them get better. The table of holy pictures and statues was decorated with plastic and silk flowers that got very dusty if Lally forgot to clean them, but no matter how dusty the altar got, all the Lawlor children knew that it was a sacred space, and they respected it.

As well as their faith and their work ethic, Lally and Robin had strong feelings about hospitality. They taught all the children, and showed through their own example, that it was very important to be kind to visitors. Whenever anyone came to the house – from the local parish priest to a tradesman coming around to repair something – they were offered tea, sandwiches, cakes and anything good that Lally had to hand. It was unheard of for someone to visit and then leave without having eaten and drunk something.

Although the many Lawlor children had plenty of space to play inside their own house or in the garden at the back, the local children mostly preferred to play out of doors, and Francis was no exception. There was a neighbourhood play area, but for the kids of the Sheriff Street area, Dublin's inner city was their real playground and they made their own fun. All year round, they would play on the street outside their homes or venture into the shopping areas of Henry Street and Moore Street for a bag of chips or an ice cream and to gape at the fancy clothes on display in the shop windows. Grand Canal Dock and the Royal Canal were both right on their doorstep, and in the summer, when it was hot, the little boys would strip off down to their underpants and dive right into the murky water, coming up with their hair plastered onto their heads like an otter and just laughing with the joy of it all. The little boys of Sheriff Street do this every summer to this day. Sheriff Street has a reputation for being rough, but for a lot of children it was a wonderful place to grow up.

When she remembered her son Francis as a little boy, Lally always said that he just loved being with other children, and wanted to be out and about the whole time. No matter how much she tried to keep him at home, he would always escape. She told me that, as a little boy, he would come home with his sleeves stiff with snot: he had been playing so hard that he never even had time to blow his nose and just wiped it on his sleeves. He would have got into trouble for that, too, if he had not been such a charmer. Lally was never able to stay cross with Francis for long, because he would just give her a cheeky grin and tell her that he loved her while she peeled off his snotty jumper to put it in the wash. Francis never came home until he was starving and needed to eat.

Francis went to the Saint Laurence O'Toole primary school on Sheriff Street, and from there to the Strand Technical College for secondary school. He was a bright student who got along well with the teachers and never got in trouble, but he was not very interested in academic study, so after the Intermediate Certificate, as it was called then, he decided to leave school. He was just 16 at the time, but anxious to get out into the world and start earning money for himself.

A lot of the people who knew Francis assumed that eventually he would find his way into the mechanics business, because he loved cars and motorbikes and always had something up on concrete blocks outside the house. As soon as he could afford it, he always had his own motorbike and his own car. From what I've heard about him, he would have loved the freedom that they represented.

Like in any large family, as the number of children grew, the older ones were often called on to help with the care of the younger ones – babysitting and keeping a general eye on their little sisters and brothers. Francis liked spending time with his younger siblings (especially with Gerard, who looked just like him) and imagined himself having a big family of his own one day. He lived at home until he joined the army in 1976, when he was 21 years old. A good friend of his from those days, Dennis Farrell (no relation to Maureen, whose maiden name was also Farrell), remembered him as universally popular and clever, with great leadership skills; the two of them qualified and took part in the passing-out ceremony together on April 4 1977.

Francis was still a bit of a chancer, however. One day the soldiers were training on the beach – it was hard work and the weather was cold. Then Francis called out that he had lost his two front teeth – he wore two false teeth in the front because of some mishap he had suffered as a child. The officer in charge told Francis to go off to the dental hospital to get himself sorted out, and the rest of the soldiers spent several fruitless hours searching the sand for the dentures. It turned out that Francis had just put them in his pocket. He enjoyed three days off at his colleagues' expense.

Francis was good at being a soldier, though, and was a natural marksman who was awarded for his talent on the day that his group of trainees passed out. This was unfortunate, in some ways, as the army decided to train him in competitive marksmanship, which meant a lot of very early mornings and less camaraderie, which was what had drawn him to the army in the first place.

The one thing that everyone says when they remember Francis is that he was very good-looking. He was tall, slender and dark, and he had thick dark eyebrows and a very hairy chest at a time when this was fashionable; in those days, the films were full of Italian-looking stars like John Travolta, George Hamilton, and Tom Selleck, with dark good looks and plenty of hair. Francis was also very interested in fashion and liked to be dapper. He spent a lot of money on clothes and often went out and about wearing a full three-piece pin-striped suit with his hair carefully combed and worn in the latest style.

Francis was very popular with girls and women because of his looks, but also because of his easy patter. He loved talking and found it very easy to talk to anyone. He could charm his way into – and out of – almost any situation. From an early age, he never had any problem finding girlfriends. He was also popular with other young men, because of his easy manner and diplomatic approach to life. Overall, Francis was a positive, forward-thinking young man. He loved people, liked to talk, and was not afraid of hard work. I think that at the time he died, in his mid-twenties, the world must have seemed like his oyster. He was really just starting out in life, and felt that anything was possible.

The story of my mother's family, the Farrells, is a little harder for me to piece together, because I spent much less time with my maternal family when I was growing up.

Maureen grew up on Attracta Road in Cabra, which is a Northside suburb about two kilometres from the north inner city and Sheriff Street. Right up until the 1920s, Cabra was still fairly rural, a place where farmers and market gardeners grew cabbages and potatoes and milked cows for the Dublin markets. Shortly after Irish independence in 1922, the government began to build housing schemes which were mostly rented by the corporation to working-class families from the inner city. For most of the people who moved to Cabra from the 1920s to the 1950s, going there represented a step up in the world because they were moving from inner city tenements with shared bathrooms, and little to no private outdoors space, to comfortable family homes with decent-sized gardens and access to good schools. By the time Maureen was born, on September 30 1957, Cabra was a good, established working-class neighbourhood with decent facilities and a strong sense of community.

Maureen was one of seven. They were: Marian, Kathleen, Maureen, William ("Willo"), Declan ("Decco"), Pat, and Séan. Her parents, Elizabeth and Paddy Farrell, were traditional Dubliners from backgrounds similar to Lally and Robin's. Like Lally, Elizabeth was an old-school housewife who took pride in caring for her children and her home. Those who knew her had great respect for her – she was considered a kind and generous woman who did a lot for others in her own quiet way.

Paddy and Elizabeth were both very religious. They went to Mass often and, like Lally, had plenty of religious statues and holy pictures in their home. Their faith was very important to them, and they did their best to raise their children according to it.

Maureen went to school locally. She was quite a confident kid when she was little, but when she was 15, she was badly injured when she was hit by a car while crossing the road on Gardiner Street in the north inner city. Her pelvis was badly damaged, and the recovery took months. Maureen's self-confidence took a big hit and so did her performance at school. She left school after the Intermediate Certificate exam, which she took at the age of 15 or 16, and got a job at a butcher's shop on Dorset Street in the north inner city, where she wrapped up people's orders and worked the till.

Maureen was really pretty: petite and slender with rosy cheeks, a fashionable blonde perm, and blue eyes. All the boys liked her. However, she did not have a lot of social confidence and was actually quite a shy young woman. By the time she had reached her teens, things had started going badly wrong in her family, too. There were some issues in the broader family with mental health and violence. Some of Maureen's relatives started getting involved in crime. Most of it was small-scale stuff but, as she grew up, some of it started getting quite serious and elements of the family were soon "well known to the gardaí", as they say. One of Maureen's brothers lost a leg on the railway track robbing trains and another served time at the Central Mental Hospital for the Criminally Insane for killing another man.

A once-happy family home became quite chaotic and, from what I have heard, it all had a big impact on Maureen. She reacted by becoming almost obsessive about hygiene and order. She washed herself all the time and changed her clothes immediately if she got a spot or a stain on something. She kept her room spotless and would get very upset if anything happened to disrupt the order that she was trying to create around her.

One thing that Maureen had in common with Francis was that she really loved fashion. She was still living at home with her parents when she and Francis started going out, so she could afford to spend much of her salary on clothes, make-up and hair products. She was always beautifully turned out. To look at her, nobody would have guessed that she was often quite anxious about the situation in her broader family.

When Maureen and Francis met, they were little more than kids. Apparently, they fell for each other straight away, and within days of getting together, the relationship was serious. They went out for about three years, and then got married when Francis was 19 and Maureen 17. The wedding was held in the church of Saint Laurence O'Toole on Sheriff Street, with Maureen in a simple white wedding dress and Francis looking proud and delighted in a suit and a pair of platform shoes. They were so young that in their wedding photos they look almost like children, just playing at being grown-ups. After the wedding, they moved into their first home as a couple, a council flat in Summerhill, which is a residential area in the north inner city that underwent a lot of redevelopment in the 1970s and was then quite a popular place for young couples starting out in life.

Maureen was anxious to become pregnant as soon as possible. All she had ever wanted was to be a mother and to raise a happy family. Unfortunately, she struggled to carry a child at first and suffered four or five miscarriages in quick succession. This was especially hard on her, but it was also tough for Francis. I think that they had both assumed that pregnancy would just happen quickly and easily, as it did for so many.

Despite this sadness in their lives, Francis and Maureen still managed to have a good time. They socialised a lot with Francis's friend from the army, Dennis, and his wife Anna, going out to pubs for a drink and spending sunny afternoons on Dollymount Strand, a popular beach in north Dublin – famously getting the wheels of Francis's red Vauxhall stuck in the sand one day, and having it pulled out by a passing rugby team.

Francis and Maureen's luck changed when they moved out of the flat in Summerhill and into a comfortable Dublin Corporation house on Cappagh Drive in Finglas. Finglas is a large suburb of north Dublin that was redeveloped in the 1950s with the creation of many new housing estates. In the

1970s, the community was a mixture of middle-aged people with older children, who had moved there in the 1950s and 60s, and young couples like my parents.

Maureen decorated her new home with meticulous attention to detail; people who knew Maureen and Francis at the time describe it as having been like a showhouse from a fancy suburb plopped down into an ordinary Northside neighbourhood.

Shortly after the move, Maureen got pregnant again, and this time the pregnancy worked out. After a few months she was blooming, and she and Francis felt confident telling their families that, at last, their longed-for baby was on the way. That baby was me. I have always known that in the short time I had with my parents, I was loved and wanted.

I was born in the Rotunda Hospital – a full-term, healthy baby girl who came into the world kicking and roaring – on 17 August 1979. The birth was very difficult and Maureen had such terrible injuries afterwards ("she was in ribbons" my Aunt Marian told me) that people assumed she would never want to give birth again. Contraception, which had been illegal or heavily regulated in Ireland for years, was much easier to get than before, and Maureen had the option of deciding how many children she wanted. I imagine the damage she had sustained to her hip as a young girl was a complicating factor.

Despite her injuries, Maureen was absolutely thrilled to be a mother and felt as though all her dreams had come true at last. I was baptised Lisa Frances Lawlor at the Church of the

Assumption in Finglas: "Lisa" because Maureen just liked the name, and "Frances" after my dad.

Like a lot of young mothers, Maureen was very anxious about getting everything right, and her obsessive behaviour around cleanliness and hygiene went up a notch. She cleaned the house from top to bottom every day. Apparently, she also changed my clothes up to five times a day and even annoyed some members of the extended family by not letting anyone touch "the babba" in case I got hurt, or in case my pretty dresses were dirtied. She did not want to socialise much at this time, in case someone brought germs into the house and made me sick, so she and Francis mostly stayed at home; their friends all assumed that they would start going out again in a little while, when they adjusted to parenthood.

Maureen washed the wheels of my pram with soap every day, and told Francis to make sure the floor was clean in his parents' house before visiting his family because she did not want to get the pram dirty. She was not shy to tell people to wash their hands before picking me up, and could be critical of my aunts, who were more relaxed about grubby little faces and sticky little hands. I know that my grandmother Lally used to get quite offended when Maureen told her to wash her hands before touching me because, having raised 12 children of her own, she felt that she knew how to take care of a baby and did not need to be told what to do by a young woman just starting out. There was a little tension sometimes. At one point my skin was red and sore because Maureen was washing me too often, and she was hurt when she was advised to be more relaxed. Had she lived to have more children I am sure that she would have learned how to unwind.

After I was born, Francis left the army and got a job working as a barman in the inner city so that he would have more time to spend with his family, and because he was getting bored with the extra work involved in competitive shooting for the army. He enjoyed the bar work and was good at it, with his ability to chat to anyone and keep up the banter. I do not know what his long-term career plans were at this stage, but as he was such a people person, I think he would have had plenty of options; he might have ended up with his own pub one day, or maybe he would have opened a mechanic's workshop, as his friends expected. As it was, Francis was proud of being able to support his little family and, like Maureen, hoped that more children would come along soon. Unfortunately, Francis's family felt that he had been very foolish to give up such a good job in the army, with plenty of opportunity for promotion, and they tended to blame Maureen for his decision. They felt that she had too much influence on him, and that he had only left the army to please her.

Maureen and Francis were so wrapped up in their lives as a couple, and in the excitement of being parents for the first time, that when Francis was not working, they generally preferred to stay at home in their own little world. Like any couple, occasionally Francis and Maureen had arguments, but they were a close unit, facing the world, and their future, together.

When I turned one, Maureen and Francis threw a big party for me at their house in Finglas and invited the family from both sides to celebrate with them. As they both had so many brothers and sisters, several of whom now also had children of their own, it must have been absolute chaos, and it would have been hard for Maureen to see everyone putting down their drinks on her shiny surfaces without using the coasters that she considered essential – but she and Francis were happy and proud to be parents and of the life they were building for themselves, and they wanted to show it off. They had no way of knowing that this was the last party they would ever have, or that this was the only birthday they would ever celebrate with me.

If everything had gone according to plan, Maureen and Francis would have gone on to build a good life for themselves, and for me. There is every reason to assume that their lives would have been happy and productive, filled with the children that Maureen longed for, and the fulfilling work life, with plenty of colleagues and banter, that Francis loved. Like anyone, they had their challenges and their vulnerabilities, but they were fine people, building the best lives for themselves that they could. It was just bad luck that they accepted a friend's invitation to the Stardust the night it went up in flames.

That last minute decision, to leave the house for a rare night out, is why, for much of my childhood, the newspapers would come to my house every year on the anniversary of the tragedy, and sometimes at Christmas too, to take pictures of and hear updates on me, the Stardust Baby. It is why, for years, I never really felt that I belonged to anyone, and why I am still trying to find answers today, as I write this book.

2

Mam and Grandad

In 1981, the year of the Stardust disaster, another disaster was unfolding all over the city of Dublin. Young people in one family after another were succumbing to heroin addiction, and the social services and medical system were not only struggling but failing to deal with it. Unemployment was rising in Ireland at that time, and there was a lot of dissatisfaction with life. The traditional values that the older people had grown up with did not seem to work for everyone anymore.

Aggressive drug dealers had started developing new markets in Dublin in the late 1970s, and they had found fertile ground for their black-market industry. For a lot of families, already teetering on the edge of serious problems, it just took one big challenge to push them right off the edge and into the deep end. For my family on both sides, the horrifying deaths of Francis and Maureen, and the fallout for everyone who had loved them, was the final straw.

Immediately after my parents' deaths, and the funeral and burial of their remains, I was brought up to Maureen's parents' home to be cared for by Elizabeth and Paddy Farrell, my maternal grandparents.

By all accounts my grandmother, Elizabeth Farrell, was a wonderful person. Those who knew her remember her as a kind, gentle lady who was deeply religious and devoted to her family and her community. God knows, she needed her faith and her positive outlook, because life had dealt her a difficult hand even before Maureen died at the Stardust. As I have already said, a number of her children had both mental health and behavioural issues, and had already been in trouble with the law. I am sure that this was heart-breaking for Paddy and Elizabeth alike. Somehow, despite all this, Elizabeth held the fort and made sure that the Farrell family home was always a welcoming place to visit.

Of course, I have no memory of the time I spent with Elizabeth, but I am sure that she was as loving and caring as she could be under very difficult circumstances. I was only with her for four weeks before the Farrell family was struck by another awful blow. Elizabeth had been absolutely devastated after the death of her daughter, Maureen. She had been a strong, healthy woman up to then, but four weeks after Maureen's death, she had a sudden heart attack and died at home. Quite literally, Elizabeth died of a broken heart. She was only 54 years old.

When Elizabeth died, the beating heart at the centre of the Farrell family, and the one person who offered that family hope of a better future, was gone. They were already numbed by their loss, and several of the family members decided that they could not care for me any longer. Shortly after Elizabeth's death, these Farrell relatives packed my bags with the few bits and pieces that had been retrieved from Maureen and Francis's home and brought me down to the Lawlor home on Sheriff Street.

I believe that the Farrells were doing the best that they could do at this time. They had just lost their mother unexpectedly, at a time when they were still actively grieving for their sister. They had already been dealing with the distress and shame of having a brother in the Central Hospital for the Criminally Insane. The creeping spectre of heroin addiction, which was already beginning to grip much of Dublin, was threatening the Farrell family, and any hope they had of beating it seemed to have been extinguished by the loss of their mother. The Farrell family was enduring a complete nightmare and, in deciding to give me up, they were absolutely doing the right thing.

Unfortunately, my grandparents Lally and Robin – who were also still reeling from the loss of their beloved son – took serious offence at the way I was handed over by my Farrell relatives. The Farrells wanted to bury their beloved mother in style, but money was tight, and they could not afford the funeral expenses, especially so soon after Maureen's death. When they gave me to the Lawlors, a financial agreement was made to help them with the costs of Elizabeth's funeral. Apparently, the Farrells said, "You can have Lisa, but our mother needs to be buried properly." Lally and Robin interpreted this as the Farrells "selling" Maureen and Francis's little girl to her relatives, and this was the very partial version of events that I grew up hearing about.

While the two families remained on civil terms, they were never very friendly after that. Now and again, throughout my childhood, Mam (as I have called her ever since I learned how to talk) or Grandad would drag up the story of how I had been "sold" by my mother's own sisters. I always hated hearing that, because it made me feel like a nuisance that neither family really wanted. I often wondered if both families would have been happier if I had never been born, as I felt as though I was the source and reason for all their disagreements.

The Lawlors often told me that, while they had been horrified by what the Farrells had done, I had been "lucky" not to be left with them because they were in no fit state to raise a little girl who had already lost so much. Sometimes I wonder how different things might have been and how they might have looked from another point of view. I found out later on that my aunt, Kathleen Farrell, and her husband, Eddie, suggested at the time that they might take me in and raise me, but by then I was already with the Lawlors, and that was that. I wish that I had known this as a child; I can see now that the stories I was told were only ever from one perspective and did not give the whole picture.

With the benefit of hindsight, I feel that both families were grieving at this time, emotions were heightened, and nobody was able to think straight. I'm sure that despite all that they were going through, they all just wanted the best for me. I do not believe that the Farrells intended to "sell" me, as Grandad often said, but that they were just trying to do the right thing by their mother, while being too upset to take care of me and also struggling with money and other issues that pre-dated both the Stardust tragedy and Elizabeth's sudden death. I believe that the Farrells were trying to do the best they could in a very difficult situation, and simply did not understand how their actions would be interpreted by the Lawlors, who were themselves emotionally devastated and hardly in any position to be objective.

Unfortunately I was never able to discuss the Lawlors with the Farrells, or vice versa, which was often very difficult for me as a child. The simple fact of the matter is that the Stardust tragedy was like a hand grenade thrown right into the middle of these two Dublin families, who were already living through what was a difficult era for the whole city. After the Stardust fire, nothing was ever right again for either side of the family.

Mam, who was in her mid-fifties at this time, had already raised a family of 12; five of my aunts and uncles – Alison and Adrian, Edel and Martin, and Denis – were still young and living at home (the younger four were still in school) but most of them were out on their own. Up until the deaths of Francis and Maureen, Mam must have been looking forward to not having to work quite so hard. My arrival, aged 18 months, put an end to all that, and diverted a lot of Mam's attention from her four youngest children, who were going through their adolescent years and still needed her support and guidance.

Mam, as I soon learned to call her, always told me that I was extremely difficult to care for at first. I was inconsolable. I wept and cried whenever she put me down. Every time someone came in the door I would look up with an expectant expression on my face, and then start to cry when I did not recognise them. I would toddle into a corner of the room and hold up my fat little arms, as though there was someone standing there and I was asking to be picked up.

Although I had a lovely room all to myself, I could not be persuaded to sleep in it, and had to sleep with my aunts Edel and Alison, who had a big room with two sets of bunk beds just for them since their older sisters had moved out. Even then, I would often wake at night screaming as though I had seen a terrible monster. The only way Mam could calm me down was to hold me in her arms and walk up and down in the dark, rubbing my back and whispering soothing words to me. It would take hours, and she was so exhausted it was hard for her to get through the day and take care of me and her four youngest children.

"The only good thing about it," she said when she told me about it later, "was that it took my mind off poor Francis and what he must have suffered in the fire. The fire used to go round and round in my head, and I was tormented with the thought of all the pain he must have been in. At least when you were screaming, I couldn't think about it. If it were not for you, Lisa, I'd be dead and buried like Elizabeth Farrell, God rest her. You gave me a reason to go on living."

Stardust Baby

* * *

One of my earliest memories is from my very first day at school, aged just four. I remember it as though it were yesterday, and I still think of it every year when I see all the little children heading off to school for the first time in their too-big uniforms.

I was walking down the street with Mam. I was dressed up in my new school uniform, a navy pinafore and string tie, all freshly purchased from Brett's drapery shop of Talbot Street in the north inner city. Going in for my uniform had been a big occasion; there had been no suggestion of hand-me-downs for me, because I was always given the best of everything.

I knew that the first day of school should have been a happy day, because I was turning into a big girl, but instead there were tears – big, fat tears – rolling down Mam's face as she walked along beside me, holding my hand. I looked up at the tears and could see them shining on her face like diamonds as they poured, unrestrained, down her cheek. She did not seem to have the energy to wipe them away.

I remember looking into her eyes and suddenly understanding how broken she was. That was one big difference between me and the other children walking down the street towards school for the first time, because their mammies looked happy, proud, and excited about the big first day. The other difference was that Mam, at about 60, was much older than the mammies bringing the other girls, who were all dressed in little pinafores exactly the same as mine. The other mammies were all in their early twenties, with fresh faces and rosy cheeks. By comparison, with her soft grey curls and her wrinkles, Mam looked like a very old lady to me, and she was always coughing, as though breathing was a big challenge for her. She was coughing then, even though she was also crying, her breath coming in big, raspy, nicotine-scented gulps between the coughs and the tears.

Mam managed to dry her tears as we drew near to the school door. She stood still for a moment and squeezed my hand while she pulled herself together. She wiped her eyes on a tissue that she removed from her pocket. Then she took a deep breath and we stepped forward together.

"Here we are, now, Lisa!" Mam said in as bright a voice as she could muster. "This is your new school, and that nice lady is your new teacher. Her name is Mrs Fahy and she's going to take great care of you. You're going to have a lovely time. You're going to make lots of new friends."

Mrs Fahy was standing by the door of the school, holding it open and smiling at the little girls filing inside. Most of the children were happy to start school and knew all about it from seeing their older siblings and cousins go to school before them. Mrs Fahy had a short, swingy dark blonde bob that moved when she turned her head, and a kind face with a big smile.

"This is my little girl, Lisa," Mam said, nudging me forward. "She's starting school today."

Immediately, the smile disappeared from Mrs Fahy's face and she looked down at me. Her eyes were open wide and her mouth was an O of horror, as though she had just seen a ghost.

As though she had finally encountered someone she had been waiting for, and dreading, for some time.

"Oh, God," Mrs Fahy said. "Is it little Lisa Lawlor? The Stardust Baby? God love her! How is she? Is she all right? Poor Lisa."

"Poor Lisa," Mam said. "God help Lisa."

Mam started to cry again. I began to wonder if it was my fault. My grandmother cried a lot, and it usually seemed to be around me and about me. Because she had told me that I was the only reason she was still alive, I was afraid that if I did anything wrong, she might lose the will to go on again. She was the bedrock of the whole family, and without her, everyone would have fallen apart.

It seems strange to remember this as clearly as I do, considering how long ago my first day at school was, and people might accuse me of imagining it or making it up, but I know with perfect clarity that this was the moment when I started to understand that my mum and daddy were really gone, and that they were never coming back, as I had imagined that they might. I had been told that they were in heaven, looking down on me. I think, until the first day of school, I believed that one day they would return from heaven, as though they had been away on holiday, and that I would have parents again, like all the other children. Seeing Mrs Fahy's shocked, sympathetic face looking down at me, and the tears of my grandmother, which were flowing freely again, I realised that this was it: heaven was forever. They were never coming back.

Mam and Grandad

Poor Lisa. God help her. She's the Stardust Baby.

I made it to the classroom, but once I got there, I went crazy. I screamed, I cried, I wet myself. The teachers tried to hug me and calm me down, but nothing they did made any difference and, small as I was, it was very difficult for them to contain me as I screamed and flailed. Over my head, I could hear them telling one another that this was to be expected, because I was the child who had lost both parents to the Stardust tragedy, three years before, and it was only natural that I was not normal. They would have to be tolerant, they said, because I was a difficult case. I realised that they saw me as damaged goods, already broken before my life had really begun.

I was too little to have the words I needed to express what I was feeling, but I still remember the horrible sensation of emptiness and yearning that took me over and controlled me then – and I remember the sudden fear that gripped me that when I got home from school Mam would be dead too, and I would be all alone.

The whole time I was at school, all I wanted to do was burst out the door and run back home, to make sure that Mam was still there and still alive. I tried to trick her into staying at home by appointing a doll for her to "mind" every day while I was at school. Mam would agree to mind the doll, and I would insist that she held the doll in her arms as I left the house.

"Don't put her down, now," I would say. "She is counting on you! She's your babba and you've got to take care of her. You won't forget, will you?"

"I'll mind her, pet," Mam said, every time. "I won't put her down for a minute."

Then I would leave the house with my Uncle Adrian, who was still in secondary school at that time. Adrian was very nice to me always, holding my hand as he led me to the primary school nearby. I ruled him like a little princess. One day, Adrian dropped the flask of tea that Mam had given me for my lunch, and rather than seeing me get upset, Adrian made himself late for school by running back to Mam with the broken flask so that she could give me something else. Of course, at the time I did not realise how generous Adrian was being; I simply accepted his kindness as my due. Adrian was a kind, smiling boy who was always available to play with at home. I will never forget how much love I got from him as a little girl.

The huge anxiety I experienced whenever I was not physically with the people I cared about caused me countless problems at school. Most of the teachers were very kind to me, and I know that huge allowances were made for me because of my tragic story, but I must have been very difficult to deal with, and I wish I could meet some of my former teachers so that I could apologise for the hassle I caused them.

I remember Miss Hynes, my teacher in first class, as especially kind and polite, as well as glamorous, with her leather skirts, matching handbags, and red lipstick. All the children in the area loved her, and I remember how excited we were when we saw her on the street, walking to or from the school under her big umbrella. Miss Hynes made a big effort to help me, with hugs, special smiles, and lots of attention. When she saw me crying, she would carry my little chair up to the top of the classroom and get me to sit down beside her. I can still remember the scent of her lipstick and her floral perfume when she leaned over me with her gentle smile. Her soft brown curls would brush my cheek. Surreptitiously, I would sneak up to her and try to sniff her neck. I am sure that she noticed, but she was always very understanding of me and my little ways.

"Don't you be worrying or crying, now," said Miss Hynes. "There's no need for any of that. You're a great girl. You're a special little girl, Lisa."

Perhaps partly because I loved Miss Hynes and her floral perfume, I developed an obsession with perfume as a child; whenever I met a woman wearing perfume, I could not rest until I had got close enough to her to smell it. I started asking Mam to get me perfume as well as dolls and toys, and when she did, I would drench myself in it. Mam started to worry that this was not quite normal, so she consulted a psychiatrist, recommended by our family doctor, who listened to her concerns, and explained that our most deep-rooted memories are inextricably intertwined with scents and smells, and that I was probably instinctively searching for my mother by seeking out the perfume that she had worn when I was little and she held me in her arms.

A special teacher came to the school to help us with our English writing skills, and we were encouraged to write poetry. This was something that I was actually quite good at, and she gave me great praise for being creative. One of my poems was good enough to win a prize, and I proudly marched home that day with the Easter egg I had been awarded. Unfortunately, my achievements in this area did not lead to any improvements in others and I continued to lag behind.

Although some of the teachers were very kind to me, I really hated school and did not understand the point of it or how education might be relevant to my life later on. My academic performance was quite poor, and mostly I was just counting down the hours until I could leave and run home to make sure that Mam was still there, or daydreaming that I would go home, and instead of Mam, my real, lovely mother would open the door and hold her arms wide for me to run in for a hug.

All of my school report cards say the same things: "Lisa is very easily distracted"; "Lisa finds it difficult to concentrate"; "Lisa is a dreamer and spends all her time looking out the window". I do not believe that I had a learning disability or any actual underlying problem that was preventing me from learning; rather, the huge levels of anxiety that I experienced every day meant that I could never concentrate on my lessons. I was always afraid that Mam and everyone I knew and cared about could vanish at any moment, or that my home would burn down while I was away, killing Mam and the rest of the family the same way my parents had been killed. I also knew that Mam was much older than my friends' mammies, and I was terrified that I would come home from school one day and find out that she had died, as my other grandmother, Elizabeth, had died. Some days at school, I could think of nothing else, and I would just sit there in class and start to weep or even to sob out loud. When the teacher asked me why I was crying, I just shook my head and refused to speak.

The teachers did their best, and were often far easier on me in some ways than they should have been, but they were not qualified to deal with my situation – and anyway, they had their hands full with large classes of children, all of whom needed attention. Many of the children in the school I attended came from families with problems of their own.

I let myself cry in school because I could not bear to do it at home, as I knew that it would just set Mam off again and then I would feel awful, because her distress would be my fault. The knowledge that she had lost the will to live after my father died, and that I was the only thing keeping her alive, was often a very heavy burden to carry.

* * *

I loved Mam most of all, and after her, I was devoted to my Aunt Edel when I was little. Edel was only 12 years older than me, so she had been nearly 14 when I arrived on the scene. When I was very small, I could not imagine life without Edel. I was always afraid that if I could not see the people who mattered to me, anything could happen, and then I might never see them again. I also felt that I was a sort of gift to Edel, a type of living doll that surely Edel always wanted to play with. I used to assure her that I would be there in the evening

31

to sleep in her bed, assuming that this was a great treat for her. If I slept in Edel's bed too often, I would start to worry that Alison, who slept in the other bunk bed, might be feeling neglected.

"I'll sleep with you next," I would assure Alison. "You can have a turn tomorrow."

The two teenage girls were very indulgent with me. I am sure that they would have preferred not to share their room with a little girl who might go poking around in their clothes or mess up their make-up, but they were always very patient and loving. Mam relied on Edel and Alison to take care of me whenever she went shopping or to Mass, and they were fantastic caregivers. I loved them both.

Despite the care I received, I remained difficult to console for years. When my Uncle Gerard married a lovely woman called Colette in 1984, I nearly spoiled the wedding by crying the whole time. Bless her, Colette held me on her lap the whole day to keep me calm, even during the wedding meal.

When I was about six, Edel was about to go on holiday to Cuba with her boyfriend Colm – it was her first grown-up holiday, and she was very excited about it. I was so upset to see her standing in the hall with all her bags packed that I threw myself at her legs and clung to them, trying to prevent her from leaving. She bent down to try to talk some sense into me, and I grabbed her face, and then her hair, and pulled as hard as I could. I screamed, hit, kicked, and bit, as my grandparents tried to pull me off poor Edel.

Mam and Grandad

Mam's faith was enormously important to her, and she also felt strongly that I should have a good religious education, and that faith and prayer would help me through my darkest times. Every night, when she was getting me ready for bed, she would sit me down in front of her, untie my hair, and give it a hundred strokes with a soft hairbrush while she taught me how to say my prayers before bedtime. I loved that ritual – the soothing feeling of the brush being pulled carefully through my long hair, and Mam's rasping, but gentle voice teaching me how to pray, "Now I lay me down to sleep."

Mam taught me that God, the angels, and my parents could hear me pray and that they would help me to stay safe during the night. Mam taught me that nothing bad could happen to me when she was there to keep me safe, so long as I kept God in my thoughts and said my prayers. I wish now that Mam had been right, because I would find out as I grew up that plenty of bad things can happen, even when you pray your heart out and even when you are with your family.

3

"God Help Her"

Mam was the first person I thought about when I opened my eyes in the morning, and the last person I prayed to God about before I went to sleep at night. I had a bittersweet relationship with her huge, hacking cough, brought on by years of heavy smoking. On the one hand, so long as I could hear Mam coughing, I knew that she was near, and that I was safe. On the other, I also knew that it meant that she was not very well, and I worried that she might die before I was a grown up and able to take care of myself.

Mam often said that I was the only thing keeping her alive, but I think that her faith played a big part, too. The dusty statues in the front room of the house that had been there when Francis was a little boy were still very important to her, and her response to any dilemma or cause of upset or sorrow was to pray about it, or to attend another Mass. She frequently dragged me to visit the grave of Matt Talbot or to say a prayer and light a candle in one of Dublin's many churches. We often visited the Pro-Cathedral, Dublin's Catholic Cathedral, to light candles. Instead of seeing a psychologist or another mental health care professional who might have been able to help her with the depression she had suffered from since Francis's death, Mam visited a nun who provided her with support from a religious perspective. Mam always seemed to be more, rather than less upset, when she came home from visiting this nun. I am sure that the nun was doing the best she could to help, but I wish that Mam had received the professional psychological help she clearly needed.

Mam went to Mass every Saturday night (that left Sunday morning free so that she could focus on cooking the huge three-course meal that everyone expected), and she always dragged me along with her. We went to the Saint Laurence O'Toole church down the road, around which so much of the community life in our area revolved. Like most children, I found Mass boring, but I knew it was important to Mam, so I would go along willingly enough. She would pray and cough her way through the ceremony; if I went in after her, I could always tell where she was from the coughing. I did enjoy the attention I got after Mass from the other older ladies, who would crowd around Mam and me and tell us both how pretty I was, and what a credit I was to her.

I listened intently to everything Mam had to say about the importance of prayer and absorbed it all like a sponge.

"Now, you have to say your prayers every day, Lisa," Mam said. "God, Jesus, and Mary can hear you, and so can your mammy and daddy, because they are up in heaven looking down at you and listening to every single word you say. When you pray, your mammy and daddy know that you are good and they feel happy."

I loved the thought that my parents could hear me when I prayed, and started to think of prayer as a sort of one-way telephone system that I could use to communicate with them. I also liked the positive attention that I received from Mam and the other adults in my life when I prayed aloud, and I enjoyed the drama and the ritual associated with our Catholic faith. Engaging in prayer enthusiastically and loudly became an important part of my identity.

As I grew up, I was increasingly aware of my image as a tragic figure: the only orphan of a disaster the whole country still talked about. The Stardust Campaign was led by Chrissie Keegan, who had lost two teenage daughters to the fire, her husband John, and their daughter Antoinette, who had survived the fire but spent time in hospital. The campaign was fighting for a new inquest and for justice for all the victims. Chrissie stayed in touch with Mam, and sometimes asked for my presence at events set up to publicise their campaign. Mam did not want to get directly involved, but she was keen to be supportive and helpful when she could, so she often made me available for the various events that were held to raise funds and attract attention to the campaign and its aims. Because I was the only orphan of the fire, there was always interest in me and in my story. The media was guaranteed to focus on me, because nothing sells papers as well as a tragic child. There were pictures of me in the paper with my new toys at Christmas every year for a number of years.

I got lots of new toys at Christmas, and again on Valentine's Day each year. I always had a day off school for the anniversary of my parents' deaths when Mam and Grandad brought me shopping for all the dolls I wanted. This shopping trip was a huge event. On the way in, we would stop off at the Pro-Cathedral to light a candle for my parents. Then we would visit two of Mam's friends – Mary Sutton and Rosie Graham – who had stalls on Moore Street, a well-known market street in the north inner city. Mary and Rosie would emerge from behind their carts to stroke my hair, tell Mam that I was beautiful, and sympathise with her on the anniversary of her loss. I would get shy and try to hide behind Mam.

"Come out, love, they won't bite," Mam would tell me. To Rosie and Mary she said, "She's not shy at home, I can guarantee you that!"

When the visit was over, Rosie and Mary would give me a piece of fruit or a flower from their stalls, and tell Mam they did not know how she coped with her grief. Mam seemed to take pride in showing her friends that she was caring for me, and that I was turning out just fine.

After spending time with Mary and Rosie, the next stop was the Bamba toy shop, where I was told I could get whatever I wanted. After I had made my choices, Mam and Grandad would stagger out of the shop weighed down with bags, and we would go back to our neighbourhood with me skipping ahead of them. Our final stop was in Grace's pub, where Mam sipped daintily on her Pils while Grandad had a pint of Guinness and I had red lemonade. The air was thick with smoke, and Mam and Grandad always lit up and added to it. The owner of the pub knew why we were there, and he would come out from behind the bar to commiserate with us.

Each year, on the Saturday closest to Valentine's Day, the anniversary of the tragedy, Mam dressed me up in a huge, pretty dress and brought me to the special commemorative Mass in Saint Laurence O'Toole's church. I would go into the church, holding my heavy velvet skirts wide, while cameras clicked all around me. My dress, new every year, was always so heavy it was hard for me to carry it on my little body, and I could hardly bend my toes in my stiff new patent leather shoes. My freshly ringleted hair bobbed up and down on my shoulders.

There was a special part of the Mass when I would toddle up to the front of the church in my heavy dress and stiff shoes, and stand on a stool to say one of the Prayers of the Faithful: "Please God, mind my mammy and daddy in heaven." All the old ladies in the church, and plenty of the young ones, would be openly crying by this stage. Someone might even wail. The newspaper photographers would take pictures. The papers made a lot of money from my story and their photographs of the tragic orphan for a number of years, but my grandparents never received a penny.

After the annual memorial Mass, scores of Mam's friends came back to the house for a sort of wake to talk about Francis and what a lovely young fellow he had been. Everyone sat around our big front room eating sandwiches and cake and drinking. Still dressed in my velvet clothes, I would be passed from one lap to the next, as though I was the package in some sort of strange game of "pass the parcel". Everyone wanted to hold me, squeeze my chubby thighs, kiss me, and tell me that they loved me and that they were sorry my parents were dead.

"God love you, pet," they all said. "You're so pretty. Your mammy and dad'd be awful proud. Will you say a prayer for me?"

I would promise them all that I would say a prayer for them, and then retreat to a corner to eat Mam's homemade cake and listen to their stories about my da and all the mischief he used to get up to when he was little.

"Come on out of there, pet," Mam would say. "Stand up and give us a twirl. Show everyone your pretty dress."

I think Mam was never so proud of me as on those social evenings after the annual Mass. Even though she was upset, I would see her smiling at me with approval from the other side of the room and enjoying the compliments she got from her friends about what a great job she was doing bringing me up. I was her little angel, and I had to do whatever I could to make her happy, because her loss was so overwhelmingly great.

"At least we don't have to worry about her when she's grown up," Mam would tell her friends, "because the government is going to take care of Lisa, and there'll be money there for her when she turns 18. Our Lisa is going to be rich; so rich she'll be able to take care of us all!"

I did not understand it at the time, but the government tribunal had stipulated that compensation was to be provided for survivors and their families, and as I was still a child, mine would be kept in a fund for me until I was old enough to access it. The legislation to arrange the compensation had taken some time – the plan was eventually unveiled in September 1985, when I was four years old. A government scheme was set up to arrange compensation for victims and their families, and anyone eligible could apply, but had to waive their right to engage in legal proceedings at a later point. As I had lost both my parents, I was eligible for more money than most.

*　*　*

When I was in first class, it was time to make my First Holy Communion. A few weeks before that, we all had to do our First Confession, so that our souls would be pure before we consumed the Body of Christ. Our teachers prepared us for it for months, teaching us all about what a sin was, and what we were supposed to say to the priest when it was our turn to be in the little box.

I was very excited about my confession, but on the actual day, I was so wound up that I completely forgot what I was supposed to say.

"Bless me Father for I have sinned…" I said, and then my mind went completely blank. I could not remember any of my sins, though I was sure there were plenty of them.

After a few minutes of me chewing on a fingernail, thinking about what to say next, the priest took pity on me and gave me a little prompt.

"Well," he said. "I'm sure you're a good girl, but maybe sometimes you're a bit bold for your mammy?"

"Oh, yeah," I said. "Yeah, that's it. I've been a bold girl for my mam and my grandad and I'm real sorry about it. I won't do it again."

"Good girl," said the priest. "Now, your penance is three Hail Marys and two Our Fathers. Will you remember to say them?"

"Oh yeah, Father," I gabbled. "That's no bother at all. You can be sure I'll do them. I'll do a grand job of them."

After my First Confession, I dashed out of the confessional and ran right up to the front of the church. Most of the children were kneeling in their places to say their penance, but Mam had taught me well and I flung myself onto my knees at the altar rail and said my prayers right in front of the altar with my hands crossed.

"Thank you, Lord," I prayed out loud. "And thank you to my mammy and my daddy, who are watching me from heaven."

"Ah, God love her," I heard one of the teachers mutter. "She would make your heart bleed."

As Mam was very religious, obviously my First Holy Communion was a very important day for her as well as for me. All of her children had made their Communions in style – and she had the framed photographs to prove it – but she was going to go all out for me.

"I'm not going to let my Lisa have anything less than the best!" Mam said. "She's only going to have one First Holy Communion and her daddy and mammy are going to miss it."

Mam had a good friend called Darkie Bolger who was a very talented seamstress, and Darkie was appointed to make my dress for the occasion. Mam bought a length of fabric imported directly from Singapore. She had gone to a shop on the south side of the city, and seen a sample that she felt was just right – white satin with little blue bows all over it in honour of the Blessed Virgin Mary, and tiny seed pearls – symbols of my innocence and purity – scattered here and there. We waited for the material for weeks until Mam started to panic that it would never arrive on time – but it did, and then Darkie worked all the hours God sent her to get my outfit ready for the big day. My outfit cost an absolute fortune.

The morning of my Communion, my hair was set in ringlets. I had little white gloves and a white rosary to match my dress, as well as white patent leather shoes with a small heel and lacy ankle socks. Darkie had made me a bag to match my dress, and I even had a matching parasol.

Mam was breathless and excited getting me into my dress.

"Don't you dare eat anything until after Mass!" she warned me. "I need you looking lovely for the photographs."

Then she got a bit tearful. She pulled out her handkerchief and started to dab at her eyes.

"You look so beautiful, Lisa," she said. "You look like a little angel. The only thing you're missing are the wings. I wish your daddy could see you now; he'd be so proud of you. I am sure that your mammy and daddy are looking down at you from heaven."

All the neighbours came out onto their front doorsteps to see me walking to Saint Agatha's church on William Street, just up the road from Sheriff Street, to make my First Holy Communion. When they admired my dress, Mam told them all about how the fabric had been flown in directly from Singapore. They all gave me money, which Mam put into her pocket to keep safe.

Mam was already tearful when we were leaving the house, and by the time we got to the church, tears were rolling freely down her face. She cried the whole way through Mass, and then all the way to the pub on Amiens Street for the family celebration afterwards.

The whole family and lots of Mam and Grandad's friends came to celebrate with me, and even my mother's family, the Farrells, came along. The men all got pints of Guinness, and there were half-pints, glasses of wine, gin, or sherry for the ladies. The children all set about eating King crisps and drinking as much lurid red TK lemonade as they could, and soon all the little ones were on a sugar high, giggling and running around the pub like mad things while the adults talked.

I sat in a corner, partly because I was still trying to be careful of my expensive new dress, but mostly because I was afraid of catching Mam's eye. She was still crying, and I felt that, somehow, it was my fault. I loved her so much. All I wanted was for Mam to live forever and to always be proud of me. I could not bear to see her cry.

Mam's children and friends gathered around her. They gave her hugs, patted the back of her hand, and kissed her soft, lined cheek. But nothing could stop her from weeping.

"At least I've got my Lisa," Mam said. "At least I've got something from Francis to remember him by."

I started to cry too, but I didn't want anyone to see me, so I pressed my face against the sticky vinyl of the padded bar seat, smelling the scent of a thousand spilled drinks and of decades of stale nicotine. I held my glass of lemonade tightly against my face, thinking that my salty tears might fall into the drink rather than onto my dress, and that nobody would notice that I was upset. Because the grown-ups were all getting tipsy at this stage, nobody did notice, and I was left alone to wonder if Mam's feelings and her endless tears were all my fault.

Before anyone could see that I was crying, my Uncle Denis stumbled into the pub. I did not know what was wrong with him, but he was not able to talk properly, and he was stumbling around all over the place. Denis wanted to be there for me on my special day, but he was in no fit state to do so. Mam was mortified.

"Denis," she hissed at him. "Will you go on home? You're making a holy show of me. This is not the time or the place."

Denis protested incoherently for a while, but Mam eventually persuaded him to leave. The atmosphere at the party changed after that, and everyone started to drift home.

"Ah Lisa," Mam said as she gathered me up from the corner. "You're after getting red lemonade on your lovely dress. And I ordered that fabric straight in from Singapore."

"I'm sorry, Mam," I sniffled. "It was an accident."

"It doesn't matter, pet," she said, giving me a hug. "The big day is over now. Let's get you home and put you to bed."

*   *   *

Because I was little, if Mam and Grandad wanted to go out, they often took me to an auntie's or uncle's house, or a friend's house, so that I could spent the night with my cousins or with the children of family friends. This was usually fun, and I enjoyed playing with the other children.

But there was one house where one of the little girls I stayed with started to molest me, sexually, from when I was about the age of five. She was five or six years older than me, and was often left to take care of me when the adults were busy. The first time she assaulted me, she told me that she was going to give me a bath and took me upstairs. I can still remember standing at the bottom of the stars, looking up at them, noticing the red and white swirls in the carpet that covered them and the dust in the heavy tasselled curtains on the landing. There was something about the situation that made me feel very anxious, but I did as I was told.

We got to the top of the stairs and she pushed me into the bathroom. My little shoes tip-tapped across the cold linoleum on the floor. She half-filled the big bath with lukewarm water, stripped off my clothes and told me to get in. Once I was in the water, she took off her own clothes and climbed in as well. She was much bigger than me, and was easily able to push me down on my back and climb on top of me. I remember a terrible feeling of panic as I strove to keep my head above water while she pushed her body against mine and started to move about.

I had a very limited understanding of what was going on, did not know what sex was, and did not know why she was doing what she did. It was frightening and confusing. I did know that it was wrong, though, because she warned me not to tell anyone and said that she would beat me up if I did.

"If you open your fuckin' mouth, I'll break your fuckin' face," she said. I knew that she meant every word.

There is no excuse for what this girl did, but I can say in mitigation that her home life was extremely difficult, and that she often saw her father beating her mother mercilessly; I believe that this girl did not get the help she needed, and that the psychological harm she suffered as a child contributed to her own violent and abusive behaviour. I would not say a word to anyone for years, but I started hating going to that particular child's house, and would make a fuss and try to persuade Mam and Grandad not to take me there. As they did not understand why I was upset, I kept on being sent there on visits, and the abuse continued. I was so frightened of this older girl that I told nobody, and learned how to disassociate during her attacks, making myself as still and as small as possible until they were over.

"God Help Her"

As my academic performance remained weak, when I was about eight, Mam arranged for a tutor to come to the house to give me private lessons, in the hope that I would catch up with the other children. Mam would never give up on me and there was always enough money to pay for anything she felt I needed.

"This is what you call 'private education'," Mam explained. "It's just to back up the normal education you get at school."

The tutor was a very pleasant young man with big glasses and a fashionable 1980s haircut. He and I would be ensconced at the huge dining table in the front room. I would sit on one side of the table, and he would sit on the other. I presume that we went through lessons together, but I mostly remember our conversations. He would ask me about my life, and I was quite happy to answer back. He was a real gentleman. When our classes were over, the tutor and Mam would have a conversation about me at the front door, while I listened from inside the house.

"God help her," Mam would say. "Is there any hope for my Lisa at all? I've been sending up prayers to Saint Jude for her, but her schoolwork isn't getting any better. She has me only destroyed with the worry. You know, I just want her to get on well after losing her parents like that. I want her to grow up to have a good job so that she can take care of herself. The way things are going in Dublin, she can't count on finding a husband to provide for her."

"God help her," is what Mam always said about me. I was so used to hearing it, I almost thought that it was part of my name.

"She's doing very well, all things considered," my tutor would reassure Mam. "Look at her; she's thriving. She's perfectly well able to speak up for herself and I can see that she's a bright girl. School results aren't everything, Mrs Lawlor. We just need to support Lisa to find out what she really likes doing, and what she's good at. She's just a little girl yet; she'll find her way."

I used to wonder if Mam and my tutor realised that I was sitting just a few yards away from them and could hear every single word. It was as though they were talking about someone else. But strangely, that didn't really bother me. I often thought about myself as though I was someone else, as though my life was a story that someone was reading to me, rather than something I lived and experienced every day. I found it easier like that.

At this time, I was very friendly with a small group of girls of about the same age as me: Natalie Sheridan, and her younger sister Amanda, who I knew from playing on the street, Rachel Sheridan (not related to Natalie and Amanda), Esther Kelly and Elaine McCann, who I knew from school. I was fond of Mrs Kelly and Mrs Sheridan too. I was especially close to Elaine, and also to her mother, who was a lovely young woman with a kind smile who always said hello to me.

However, despite having friends on the street and in class, when I was about nine, I decided that I wanted to go to a different primary school, and Mam enrolled me in a new school which my cousins attended. I hoped that this would be a fresh start for me, but my academic performance remained weak.

Outside of the house, I was always flitting around, but at home, Mam was the central point around which my entire life still revolved. Like my father and his siblings before me, I loved Mam's cooking. By the time I was growing up in the 1980s, very few Dublin housewives still wanted the traditional cuts of meat that Mam favoured, doing the rounds of the old-school butcher shops to buy exactly what she wanted. Now everyone was eating pizza and spaghetti bolognese, and it was harder than before for Mam to find the ingredients she needed to feed us like the "proper" Dubliners we were. At the weekends, and sometimes after school, I would trail around the shops with Mam. Often the shop-owners would give me a lollipop in a lurid shade of green or red or yellow.

"There you go, pet," they would say. "Aren't you a great little girl to help your granny?"

"Oh," Mam would say, "sure, Lisa do give me a reason to go on living. She's the reason why I still get up in the mornings. I'd be dead if it wasn't for her."

"Ah, God bless her," they'd say. "Isn't it awful hard?"

Then I would get another lollipop, and sometimes maybe the shopkeeper would come around from behind the counter to give me a sentimental kiss and tell me that I was an angel.

I learned at a very early age that if everyone felt sorry for you, they gave you nice things. I had also begun to realise that the reason why I had so many toys and pretty things was because of what had happened to my parents ("Your mammy and daddy are in heaven, Lisa – now, do you like the pretty dolly? Do you want to try on your lovely new dress?") – and I had also started to absorb the lesson that the best way to make people feel better was to buy them with money and expensive presents.

Sometimes the meals Mam prepared with the special cuts of meat she brought home did not look very appetising, but they always tasted delicious, because she could make a wonderful dinner out of anything. Often Mam and I would bake a cake – gur cake, Victoria sponge, coconut cake, Bakewell tart – together when I came home from school; I loved the smell of the vanilla essence, and the gritty feeling of the desiccated coconut between my fingers. Mam made me feel very proud of my lopsided baked creations. She taught me how to knit, too, although I have long since forgotten.

Although we had our happy times, I do not think that Mam was ever really content again after Francis died. She could not cope with the knowledge that she was still living her life when her young son had been taken in his prime, through no fault of his own. She said that she wished she could have been taken instead of him; that it was not fair that Francis, who still had so much to give the world, had died before he could really be fulfilled. When I asked her what had happened that terrible night, Mam always told me that both of my parents had died of smoke inhalation, and were "dead before they hit the ground". I don't know if she had been told this by the authorities, or if she just had to believe it to keep herself sane.

Mam's physical and emotional health declined steadily throughout my childhood, and she made frequent visits to the local doctor, Doctor Flood, who had a practice on Rutledge Place. Mam had great faith in Doctor Flood.

"Come on, Lisa," Mam would say. "I've an awful bad chest on me. We're going up to see Doctor Flood so that she can prescribe me a tonic."

Mam would pull on her heavy sheepskin coat and her fur-lined boots and help me to put on my own little coat, and finally she put on her own headscarf and tied it under her chin before we left.

Doctor Flood was a famous local eccentric, rumoured to live in the upmarket Gresham Hotel on O'Connoll Street. The locals held her, and her medical expertise, in high regard, partly because she was generally happy to prescribe whatever medication the patients felt they needed.

Doctor Flood's clinic was in an old Georgian building. Mam and I spent countless hours sitting on the stiff-backed chairs in her waiting room – Mam often smoked as she waited and tipped her ash into one of the many steak and kidney pie tins that Doctor Flood left out for her patients to use as ashtrays, regularly almost overflowing with butts, ash, and spent matches.

Eventually, it would be our turn to go in. Mam would take her cigarette from her mouth and use the sharp edge of her thumbnail to deftly flick the ash and ember from her cigarette into the tin, before storing what was left of the cigarette in her left-hand pocket; I remember the woollen edge of the pocket's nicotine-yellow stain as a result of this habit.

Doctor Flood always brought her pet poodle to work, and I would pet the dog and play with it while she listened to Mam's chest. I also liked staring at Doctor Flood, who was a source of fascination to me. She was an older lady, still very glamorous, with her blonde hair tied up in a large bun on the top of her head, and plenty of make-up.

"Hello Lisa," she would say to me, looking down at me through the glasses on the end of her nose. "How are you today? Are you helping your granny?"

"I am, yeah," I would say. "Her cough is awful bad today, Doctor Flood. She do have a terrible chest on her."

"Well, then," she would answer. "We'll have to see what we can do about that."

Although I had been told that Doctor Flood lived in the Gresham Hotel, I was convinced that she really lived in her clinic, and thought that her examination table was her bed. I regarded her with a type of awe, and listened acutely when she asked Mam how I was doing; they both agreed that I needed all the help that God could send me, because I had been dealt such a dreadful hand in life.

Mam fretted that I was too thin, but when she asked Dr Flood if I was all right, she was assured that I was in perfect health. Unconvinced by this, and certain that I had worms, Mam periodically subjected me to "worm cakes", which were an old-fashioned remedy she purchased from one of the few chemist's shops that still stocked them. Mam had been brought up with worm cakes and she had complete faith in them and in their ability to keep children healthy and worm-free. They tasted absolutely revolting and I never wanted to eat them, but Mam would stand over me and make sure that it all went down.

"At least you won't have worms now, pet," Mam would say. "That's one thing we don't need to worry about."

Because she felt so sorry for me, the little girl with no parents, Mam tried to make my childhood as good as it could be by spending every extra penny she had on expensive clothes and toys for me. Where most little girls might have three or four dolls, I must have had hundreds. It was very hard for me to choose a favourite because I had so many of them. They were lined up in rows in my room, along with my prams, doll's houses, teddies, and other things.

It was as though I had a birthday every week, and when it was my actual birthday, I was given even more. When I needed new clothes, Mam would never go to Dunnes or Penney's or any of the reasonably priced outlets that most mothers used to buy clothes for their children. Instead, I wore expensive little velvet dresses from luxury shops, cut in a style that had been fashionable when Mam herself was young. Even my underwear was special, made from high-quality materials and edged with lace.

When my little cousins protested that it was not fair that I was given so much more than them, they were told that I needed more presents that they did because I was an orphan, the Stardust Baby. I was given everything Mam thought I wanted – but the only thing I really craved was the one thing I could never have: my parents.

Inevitably, my preferential treatment in the family started to cause tension. Now that I am an adult woman with children of my own, I can completely understand the situation from both points of view. Mam felt that I needed special treatment because both my parents had died in such a terrible way – but my young cousins could not even remember Francis and Maureen, and all they could see was that our grandparents gave me everything I wanted, while they had to make do with the small toys and bits and pieces that were all Mam and Grandad could afford to give them after they had lavished so much money on me.

Some of my cousins also had their own difficulties to deal with at home: one of my aunts suffered terrible domestic violence at the hands of her husband, and it was terrifying for the children, hearing her scream as they huddled on the stairs and wondered if Mammy was going to survive the latest beating. I know because there were times I huddled there with them.

As we all got older and my cousins became increasingly aware of the fact that I was Mam's favourite, a certain amount of irritation filtered into our relationship. My cousins would sneer at me and tell me that I was not nearly as special as I thought I was, and I would pull myself up to my full height and say that if I was not special, then how come I had hundreds of dollies and designer clothes, when they had none.

I was sure that I was special because Mam always did what I wanted, and she often made sure that others did too. I remember causing a huge scene one day because I did not have nappies for my baby doll; to keep me quiet, Mam told Alison to stop what she was doing and go straight to the supermarket to get some.

"Get them quick before my heart is broke here this evening," Mam said.

Alison went straight away because nobody wanted to upset Mam. I knew that I could always get everything I wanted, just by threatening to cry.

I can completely understand now that this level of indulgence towards my every whim was bound to cause friction with the rest of the family – and it did. Honestly, I think that we were all children just being children and that the situation was not managed by the adults as well as it could have been. If someone had sat us all down and explained that yes, I had more toys than my cousins, but then I had no sisters and brothers to play with and no mammy or daddy, I think my cousins would have understood. I could also have been encouraged to share my toys more with them, and it would not have hurt me to do without the designer clothes. We really just needed a grown-up to pay some attention to what was going on and listen to all our concerns, but the grown-ups in our lives were distracted by other things.

Part of the problem was that some of Mam's children, my aunts and uncles, had started to feel some resentment about me too.

When they were growing up, Mam and Grandad had 12 children. Grandad had a good job and earned decent money, but between the cost and the logistics, taking them all on holiday had really been out of the question; a day out at Dollymount Strand was the most they could hope for. Now that Mam and Grandad were only rearing me, I got taken on holiday to Blackpool in England, where I was bought all the Blackpool rock I could eat, and taken to the amusement park as often as I wanted, or to Prestatyn in Wales to stay at Pontin's Holiday Park.

When my aunts and uncles were young, they had not been able to do many organised extra-curricular activities; there were so many of them it would have been too expensive. I was allowed to join whatever I wanted, and leave as soon as I got bored, even if Mam had just spent lots of money on new outfits and equipment for me – that is what happened with the Brownies, with the bowling team I joined, and with countless other activities that I just picked up and dropped as the whim took me. To the rest of the family, I must have seemed like a spoiled, ungrateful brat; especially, perhaps, to the ones who were still young and living at home when Francis died.

Sometimes Mam just needed a break from taking care of me, and I would be sent to stay with one or other of my aunts, where I often misbehaved, and screamed and cried to be allowed home. Mam always defended me and, eventually, I always got my way. She would always take my part whenever someone complained about my behaviour, and always told me that I had done nothing wrong.

"You just don't mind them," Mam said. "They're just jealous of you. You hold your head high, Lisa! You've got finesse. You've got a look about you that's just angelic, and it'll see you through life all right. You just listen to me, and you won't go wrong."

Mam never guessed that I was still being abused by the older child who had started molesting me when I was just five years old. By the time I reached the age of about 11, and had become bigger and stronger, the abuse had started to taper off. Still, I never felt safe around that girl, or indeed around anyone. If someone who Mam trusted absolutely could do such things to me, I thought, then it could happen with anyone. I was always on high alert, nervous and jumpy, and very anxious when anyone made physical contact with me, even in a benign and affectionate way. To this day, I find close physical contact with other women difficult, as it brings back such painful memories. On holidays with friends, when it would be convenient sometimes to double up in a large hotel bed, I just cannot bring myself to do it and prefer to sleep on the floor.

The one person I always loved staying with was Denis's girlfriend Babs. Babs and Denis had a little girl called Karen, almost the same age as me, and Babs sometimes collected me and brought me over to her house for the weekend, where we children could play and just have fun. Babs was great – a small, energetic woman who was always perfectly dressed, coiffed, and made-up. She loved Denis, but she also had a strong sense of self-preservation and she had decided, with good reason, that she did not want to live with him.

Apart from the loss of Francis, which was a dark cloud that always seemed to hover above our family, there was another darkness that I was only just beginning to be aware of. The heroin epidemic, which had just begun to take a dreadful hold over Dublin when my parents died, was now entrenched in our own family. I know now that the reason why Denis had been stumbling and falling around on the day of my First Holy Communion was that he was already addicted. Denis was the first, but he would not be the last, of the Lawlors to fall prey to the Dublin heroin pandemic.

Now, obviously, I cannot say that if the Stardust tragedy had never happened, nobody in my family would have become addicted to heroin – it was everywhere in those days, and plenty of families of all sorts suffered from it. However, what I can say with certainty is that if Mam had not been distracted by her own grief – which appeared to be as deep and as endless as the sea – and with her responsibilities towards me, then things would not have become as bad as they did. She would have realised earlier what was happening to some of her adult children, and she might have had the emotional strength she needed to intervene.

Perhaps heroin would still have entered the family, but our problems would have been handled so much better, and would have been much less severe, if the Stardust fire had never happened.

By the time I was nine years old, two of my aunts and uncles were heroin addicts. My Uncle Denis, who had started taking heroin in around 1983, was completely changed by his addiction by the end of the decade. He had been forced to move back home because he was no longer working – or even able to work. Denis was a good person, but heroin changed him the way it changes everybody who starts taking it. He fooled himself into thinking that he could pass off his behaviour as being the result of one pint too many and would stagger around to our house late at night and fall in the door, slurring his words and stumbling.

"What the hell is wrong with you?" Grandad would shout. Grandad was no fool, and he knew exactly what was going on. "What the fuck are you after doing to yourself?"

"I'm grand," Denis would mumble. "I just had a couple pints is all. D'you've any money you can give me a lend of?"

"Come on, then!" Grandad would say. "We'll go back down to the pub and you can get me a couple of pints of whatever you're after having."

Then Denis would slump down onto the floor and Grandad would go mad.

I remember coming home from school one day and finding Denis in the kitchen with one of his friends. He was in a state of confusion. He was pouring sugar into the teapot and stumbling around the room, knocking everything over.

"For God's sake, Denis," Mam said. "What's wrong with you?"

"He's after taking a tablet last night, Mrs Lawlor," Denis's friend said. "He's not very well at the moment."

Denis's friend left, and Mam just sat down and buried her face in her hands and started to cry.

"What's wrong with him, Mam?" I asked. "Is Denis going to be all right?"

Mam's shoulders shook with her sobs.

"He's just tired," Mam said. "He'll be all right."

Denis fell asleep and did not wake again until the next day when he could remember absolutely nothing about what he had been doing.

The bottom line, so far as Mam and Grandad were concerned, was that Denis was their son, so they did not kick him out, even though he stole from them continuously. It might have been better for Denis if they had told him to go and live somewhere else, but they were just doing the best they could in the face of an implacable adversary.

Not long after that, my Aunt Alison had to take me somewhere in a taxi. We had not been in it long when Alison slumped over to the side, leaning on me. Her eyes were half-closed and her mouth was half-open.

"Ah no," I thought. "Not her too. Here we go again."

I was only 10 years old, but I already knew what people looked like when they were on heroin. Soon Alison's life was being destroyed by the heroin, just as Denis's had been. She was unable to think straight and was prepared to do anything so long as she got her fix. She was a beautiful girl, 23 years old. If Mam's heart had not already been broken, it would have broken all over again.

Mam took comfort from the fact that several of her children were actually doing fine: Don was in the army, Edel worked in a solicitor's office, and Carol had her own Irish dancing school. I studied Irish dancing with Carol and even entered a few competitions. Poor Carol was mortified when a number of her students competed in a contest at Dublin's Mansion House, where the Lord Mayor lived, the day Denis was arrested at Dun Laoghaire ferry port for possession of heroin. It was all over the newspapers, and everyone knew about it. Carol told me to dance with my head held high and not let anyone see how upset and embarrassed we were. Not long after that, Denis was sentenced to five years in prison.

I was aware of the tension between the Farrell and the Lawlor families, and I was fiercely loyal to Mam, but I still wanted to know my mother's family. Now that I was older, I knew how to get to the Farrells' house on my own. Often, when I had a bit of pocket money, I used it to take the bus up to Cabra so that I could visit the Farrells. I hoped that by knowing them, I would feel a deeper sense of connection to my mother, and that one day I might feel as though I fitted in there.

Sometimes I would knock on the door and find that there was no one there, so I would have to go all the way back home again. Other times, one of my uncles would let me in; Decco, Willo, and Séan were all still living at home.

I have to say that my Farrell uncles were kind to me and I believe that their hearts were in the right place. They would sit me down at the kitchen table, give me a biscuit, and ask me how

I was. I did not realise it at the time, but all three of them were also on heroin, and their addiction was steadily growing worse.

The Farrells' problems did not start with the Stardust fire, but the loss of Maureen and then Elizabeth in such a short space of time certainly made everything worse than it might otherwise have been. Elizabeth had been the pillar of their family, and with her gone, there was little hope that they would manage to lead a normal life.

My grandfather, Paddy Farrell, had never really recovered after the loss of his daughter and his wife in rapid succession. He had been a very hard worker, but after his retirement, he did almost nothing other than sit in his easy chair in the front room, watching the telly or looking out the window while he smoked, his glasses so fogged up that I could hardly see his eyes behind them. He smoked roll-ups and I would watch in fascination as he smoked them down until there was nothing left. I wondered how he managed not to burn himself.

Whenever I came into the room, my Farrell grandfather would look at me with a sort of wonder in his eyes.

"Jaysus," Paddy would say. "You're the spitting image of my Maureen. It's like my Maureen came down from heaven to visit me."

"Will I do some Irish dancing for you, Granda?" I would ask.

Paddy would agree that he would like to see me dancing, but after a few minutes of my jigs and reels, he had always had enough.

"Will you sit down, love?" he would ask. "You'll wear out my oil cloth with all your leppin' about."

Paddy's eyes would fill with tears as he watched me walk around. He would repeat the phrase "You're the spitting image of my Maureen" at intervals for the duration of my visit, and rarely said much else to me. Grief had aged him before his time and while I am sure that he wished me nothing but the best, I was a living reminder to him of all that he had lost. He seemed to have very few interests in life – just smoking and growing cabbages in his garden.

My feeling of not belonging anywhere filtered into my behaviour at school. I had a few little friends but, just like at home with my extended family, I always felt that I had to pay them in some way to keep them liking me. I also still found it very difficult to concentrate in class, and because the teachers felt sorry for me (and talked about my pitiful situation among themselves over my head) they did not push me to achieve all I could, and I drifted along, unaware, and unable to really care, that I was selling myself short.

As time passed, Mam's grief and depression got worse, rather than better. I think that in the years shortly after Francis's death, she benefitted a lot from all the sympathy and attention she received from her friends, who were all desperately sorry for her. But time moves on and, inevitably, people could not remain available to provide the same level of support many years after the tragedy. Then, the few emotional reserves that Mam had left were used up by the sorrow, grief, and shame she felt around the heroin addiction of two of her adult children, and their growing criminal records.

Denis got out of prison and came home. Mam was doing her best to help him get off the drugs and return to a normal life. Despite his troubles, Denis was a kind and loving man, and he was often good fun to have around. In prison, he had picked up the habit of reading, and he always had a book on the go. People generally liked Denis, because of his gentle manner, his lively sense of humour, and his good looks – he was very proud of his blond hair, which he wore with a fashionable quiff. His new girlfriend, Louise, lived up the road and Denis and Louise had two little girls called Lauren and Claudine. I called over to Louise all the time and begged her to let me take Lauren out in her pram. When she said "yes" I would wheel the baby about proudly, like a little granny.

Denis helped out a lot too: he liked everything to be neat and tidy and he would spend hours scrubbing and cleaning the house and even doing things like bleaching the grout in the bathroom – this may have been a habit he acquired behind bars.

One day Denis was cleaning the hall outside the shower room where I was having a wash. When I started getting dressed, I noticed something strange.

"There's some blood in my panties," I said to Denis, when I got out of the shower. "What should I do about it?"

Denis stopped cleaning for a minute and looked at me in consternation.

"Jesus, Lisa, I don't know," he said eventually. "Could you put a plaster on it?"

"Where would I stick the plaster, though?" I asked in confusion.

Denis started to laugh affectionately, and then I started to laugh. Soon we were both laughing so hard we had to hold on to each other to stand up. "I think you'll be okay, Lisa," he said eventually. "You'd better have a chat about it with one of your aunties."

Denis was the first person I told about getting my period, because I had no idea what was going on, or that girls did not usually like to discuss these matters with their male relatives. Mam was really old-fashioned when it came to talking about bodily functions, and she had not prepared me for adolescence. Even after my period started, I knew that it was not something she would ever be prepared to discuss with me directly. One of my aunties sorted me out with what she referred to as "mammy nappies" and the only reference Mam ever made to my period was to give me a little wink and tell me that she had my white jeans cleaned and pressed.

In September 1993, just as I was starting my final year of primary school, the Stardust Memorial Park was opened in Coolock in memory of all those who died. The Lord Mayor of Dublin, Tomás MacGiolla, performed the opening ceremony, and all the survivors, and the families of those who had died, came up for it. Members of the Stardust Campaign for justice were there, and Chrissie and Antoinette Keegan spoke about the work that they were doing. Everyone cried as the Lord Mayor pronounced the park open. The newspapers had sent reporters and photographers, and I remember the photographers turning to face me and then dropping to their knees to take my photograph as the words "Stardust Baby" swept through the crowd.

"Hiya Lisa," a photographer called over. "Can you look at the camera for us, love?"

All the cameras started to click as I gave a nervous smile. The whole crowd turned to stare at me and I felt as though I was special. Mam had probably known that this would happen, and as usual she had made sure that I was wearing a pretty dress for the occasion, so that I would reflect well on the family when the newspapers came out the following day.

By the time I was getting ready for my Confirmation, and to leave primary school, Mam was really suffering. Whereas my First Holy Communion had been a source of excitement, pride and joy to her, she said that she simply could not face my Confirmation. I went through the ceremony with my class-mates without Mam there to see me, although Grandad and Carol came. Mam stayed at home with her silent plaster saints, weeping in the front room and praying for help to a God who seemed not to be listening.

While Mam cried at home, I cried at the church, because even though I understood why, it hurt me that she was not there.

4

A Difficult Girl

A lot of things happened around the time I turned 13: our lovely old house was the subject of a compulsory purchase order, so we had to move home; Grandad was now semi-retired and spending a lot more time in the house than ever before; I started secondary school, and adolescence struck me like a runaway train.

All of these things posed quite a challenge, and not just to me, but also to my grandparents, who were getting older and finding the responsibility of raising a teenage girl increasingly tiring.

First of all, the corporation was planning to develop the land on which our house was built, so Mam and Grandad had no choice but to sell up and move out of the home where they had lived all their married life. This big change was really tough on both of them, but especially on Mam, whose whole life revolved around her home, which was her pride and joy. Grandad had always been a hard worker; he had spent a lot of his time at work, and socialising with the people he knew from there, so he had many contacts outside the house. It was different for Mam. All of her friends lived in the area, and she was just up the road from the church of Saint Laurence O'Toole, which was a huge part of her life. For her, losing her house was a sort of bereavement.

Mam and Grandad decided to move to Marino, a Northside suburb a few kilometres away from the Sheriff Street area that had been their home for so long. Marino was a residential neighbourhood that had been built in the 1920s and 30s to accommodate young families from the inner city. It still had a family atmosphere and was closely linked to the north inner city, where most of the people in Marino had roots. Several of my aunts and uncles were already living in the area and raising their children there. With the money from the old house, Mam and Dad would be able to buy a comfortable new home, and they thought they would enjoy being close to so many of their grandchildren and watching them grow up.

The house that Mam and Grandad bought was on 57 Croydon Park Avenue. A year after we moved in, my Uncle Martin moved in just two doors down with his girlfriend Alison (Mam wanted them to get married, but for some reason Martin was unwilling). My Aunt Carol lived across the road, and my Aunt Evelyne lived around the corner.

Martin had a good job as a forklift driver in a warehouse on the outskirts of the city. Evelyne had a child-minding service at home, and Carol had given up teaching Irish dancing and was working in a childcare facility in the city centre; they were all well-integrated into the area and gave every impression of having happy and fulfilling lives. They all told Mam that now that they were closer, they would be able to take a more active role in helping her to raise me and she said that she was glad of the support. Mothering a child was taking more out of her than it used to now she was getting older.

We called the new place the White House because it was painted all in white outside. It had a porch that led into a fairly wide hall, two reception rooms – we would use one as a bedroom – and a big kitchen extension and conservatory at the back that gave onto quite a large garden encircled with high walls. Upstairs there were three bedrooms and a bathroom.

Mam could not bear to part with any of the heavy old furniture from Seville Place, so it was crammed into the new house, even though it did not quite fit. Heavy mahogany sideboards and tables that had looked just right in the high-ceilinged Georgian rooms of our old house looked too big and incongruous in this new setting. The table was so big in the smaller new kitchen that it looked out of proportion.

Mam's beloved plaster saints were set up on top of Grandad's safe in the entrance hall downstairs, where they seemed to keep a watchful eye on all of the comings and goings. It felt like a bit of a downgrade from the honoured position they had held in the rarely-used front room of the old house, where they had chiefly watched over special occasions and exalted visitors like the priest. There was also a Bible on top of the safe, and Grandad took to putting the weekly Lotto ticket between its pages in the hope that it would help him to win – of course, it never did, but he always seemed to enjoy the weekly ritual.

Mam tried to recreate the feeling of the old house with painted textured wallpaper and net curtains. Although both Mam and Grandad did their best to surround themselves with their familiar bits and pieces, the new house never felt the same, and they never stopped missing the old one or feeling upset that the government was able to take it from them, just like that. I think that part of Mam worried that Francis might not know where they were when he looked down from heaven, and that she felt further away from him now that we had moved out of the inner city where he had grown up.

Mam had found the move to Marino extremely stressful; it had aged her, and the depression that she had been struggling with since Francis died continued to get worse. With the loss of her old house, where Francis had grown up, she felt that another part of him had been taken from her, another link with him had gone. Without easy access to her friends and all the familiar places where she was used to going, she seemed to retreat inside herself and, with each day that passed, to become a little sadder, greyer, and older.

I had the big bedroom at the front of the house, showing everyone who was the most privileged member of the family. It had built-in wardrobes and a wine-coloured carpet and curtains. It was a typical girl's room. I loved cosmetics and perfume, and my dressing table was always cluttered with my bits and pieces, while clothes and hair accessories hung from every available surface.

My room was my sanctuary, where I could listen to Take That and Celine Dion, drench myself in perfume, and imagine what life would be like when I could leave school. I spent endless hours in front of the mirror examining my face in minute detail and practising a sexy swoosh with my long, permed hair. Mam was prepared to pay for as many perms as I wanted, and I spent a lot of her money at the hairdresser getting the latest styles. She still gave me everything I asked for, although increasingly she told me to be discreet about it, because it might annoy the rest of the family if they knew how much I had. "They don't need to know everything, Lisa," she said. "You don't have to tell them."

I still loved Mam dearly and enjoyed doing things with her. I remember watching endless reruns of the 80s show *Hart to Hart*, which was one of her favourites, now relegated to daytime TV. Mam would settle herself into her usual kitchen chair to watch the characters solve crimes on the smaller set we kept in the kitchen. I would come up behind her and stretch my arms around her – she was a big, soft pillow of a woman now: all those years of baking and eating cakes had expanded her waistline – and kiss her just behind her ear on her blue-rinse curls. I loved the velvety feel of her soft, wrinkled skin and the springiness of her set curls against my face. Then I would settle down on a chair beside her, snuggled against her comforting, well-upholstered side and breathing in the mingled scents of her cigarettes and Lifebuoy soap, to watch the show with her. Mam would take my thin hand in her soft, wrinkled one and hold it, and for a while we would be at peace and happy together. Those are some of the happiest memories I have from that time of my life.

But Mam was much more tired than before. Her long history of smoking was taking its toll on her health, as was the depression that had blighted her life ever since Francis died. Moving away from the inner city had removed her from the local parish church that she loved, her familiar routes and rituals, and her network of old friends, who had always been on hand to tell her that she was doing a wonderful thing, raising her granddaughter after her son's tragic death.

Now she went to Mass in Marino, where she hardly knew anyone, and she saw her friends much less often than before. She still went into town once or twice a week to have a drink in Lloyd's pub on Amiens Street, but as time passed, her friends were not always able to come out, and these meet-ups became even less frequent although she still had great friends in the inner city. Mam was increasingly left alone with her thoughts, sorrows, regrets, and worries for the future, and with the hacking cough that often left her so short of breath that she had to sit down to recover.

I was enrolled in the Dominican College convent school for girls on Griffith Avenue together with my cousin Mary – one of my Aunt Mary's daughters. Aunt Mary had a good job as a legal secretary, and she was ambitious for her children. I think that Mam and Aunt Mary both hoped that, by going to school with Mary, I would start to find my way and improve at my studies.

A Difficult Girl

Mary was a great girl, with a big smile, a lively sense of humour, and natural intelligence and wit by the bucketload. At this stage in my life, she was not just my cousin, but also my best friend. I told her everything, and together we listened to the popular music of the time and talked about boys. I was so glad that we would be going to the same school together, because it was much bigger than the little primary school I had attended, and I would have found the crowds of uniformed girls very daunting without her.

Despite my cousin's reassuring presence, I was not at all happy about starting secondary school. Much as I had disliked primary school, it had been familiar and the teachers were all very kind and understood me; when I performed poorly they all knew that little could be expected of me because of my tragic past. Now, the prospect of secondary school terrified me: the huge crowds of girls I had never met before; the new subjects; teachers who did not know me and would not know that the Stardust Baby could not be held to the same standard as others. My weak performance in primary school meant that I had fallen far behind the other children, and I was afraid that the other girls would think that I was stupid. What was even more upsetting was the fact that my performance at school was much worse than my cousin Mary's, inevitably inviting comparisons that would not be flattering to me.

Mary and I were so close in age – there were just a few months between us – that we were always compared to one another. That had not mattered when we were both little, cute girls – but now Mary was a bright, socially confident, academ-ically talented girl, while I was failing at most subjects and had extremely low self-esteem that often manifested as surliness. It was not Mary's fault, but I compared myself to her and felt terribly inadequate, while sometimes my aunts and uncles advised me to follow her example and try to work harder. They meant well, but I interpreted their words as meaning that they thought I was stupid.

"Don't mind them, Lisa," Mam would say. "They'll come around. Just be patient. You just need to find your own way in life, and then they'll see what a great girl you are."

I reasoned that I did not need to do well in school, because all I wanted in life was to be a mother, and you do not learn how to mother from a book. I had always loved babies – I begged to hold and play with any baby I ever encountered – and dreamed of the day when I would have a large family of my own. While this dream was real and heartfelt, it was also the opt-out clause I needed to excuse my weak academic performance.

Most of all, though, I was still afraid that one day I would go to school, and Mam would have died. Because she'd always said that I was the only thing keeping her alive, now that she was getting older, I felt that if I did not stay with her all the time, she might die at any moment. I had constant fantasies about arriving home from school to find the police waiting to tell me that Mam had suffered a heart attack while she was doing her shopping on Meath Street, or that she had keeled over at home. I could imagine these scenarios so vividly, I almost convinced myself they were real. Just like in primary school, in secondary I often burst into uncontrollable tears because I was afraid of Mam dying. It was worse now, however, because I knew that this behaviour was not appropriate for a big girl of 13, and I expected to get in trouble for it, or to be bullied.

Because I knew that I was vulnerable to being picked on or bullied by the other students, I decided to protect myself by becoming the class clown. I was extremely disruptive in class, laughing and joking and doing my best to encourage the other students to misbehave. I never did my homework, and just shrugged and rolled my eyes when the teachers asked me to explain myself. Because of my lack of focus and the fact that I had already fallen so far behind, I was put in a class called "Special English" which provided remedial teaching to students who needed some extra help. There were six of us in the class in total, and I did whatever I could to make sure that none of us learned a thing.

Even though I must have been a complete pain in the neck, some of the teachers were very kind to me because they knew about my tragic past and felt sorry for me. On the days when I couldn't stop crying, they would ask me what was wrong and try to get me to settle down. My form tutor was a lady called Miss Bisset. She was exceptionally kind. She attempted to explain to me that it was in my interest to try to learn, because that way I would acquire the skills I needed to take care of myself. I would nod and smile at her and tell her that I would try to do better, but I ignored her advice. I was completely unable to plan for the future, or even to imagine it. All I knew was that I did not want to be at school. All I wanted was to sit at home with my grandmother. Sometimes I would get myself into such a state at school that I would make myself sick, and my form teacher would have to ring Mam and let her know that someone had to come and bring me home.

Mam was in her mid-sixties now, and even without her own troubles, it would have been difficult for her to deal with a stroppy teenager. I was growing up, and I was increasingly wilful. She did her best to encourage me to stay in school, often bribing me with the promise of a day off, if only I would go today. She did her best to engage positively with the school. When it was time for the parent-teacher meetings, she would tie her scarf firmly under her chin, squeeze her feet into her fur boots, and line up alongside the much younger parents of my classmates to hear one teacher after another tell her that I was not managing to reach my potential. Just as in primary school, there was no actual reason for me to fail to learn. There was nothing wrong with me, except that I did not want to be there, and my mind was always somewhere else.

Much as I loved Mam, I was embarrassed to know that she was going to those meetings, because usually mothers went rather than grannies and I wanted to be like the other girls. I was also embarrassed on my own behalf because I knew that she loved me and wanted to be proud of me, and that my weak academic performance was extremely disappointing to her, especially when my cousin was doing so much better than me.

"If you put your mind to it, you could get a good Leaving Certificate and go to college," Mam would say, coaxingly. "Then you'd be able to get a good job. You could be a nurse or something. Maybe a legal secretary like your auntie…"

Mam had had very little education herself, but she knew how important it was, and she could see how, these days, young people needed a good Leaving Certificate to get on in life. It was not like in her generation when youngsters left school early and did apprenticeships to get them ready for work. Of course, I paid her no attention.

Sometimes Mam could not cope with another round of disappointing feedback from my teachers, and she asked one of my aunts to go instead. That was almost worse, because I knew that she was waiting anxiously at home for the news, hoping against hope that I would have shown some progress. I was also embarrassed at the thought of my aunties knowing how poorly I was doing and presumably telling everyone else in the family about it, too.

Like any teenager, I wanted to push against the restrictions placed on me by my caregivers and to expand my horizons. Because I did not want to upset Mam, I reserved my most rebellious attitude for my aunts and uncles, who tried with varying degrees of success, and diverse motivations, to help Mam and Grandad and be parental figures to me. Our relationship, which was already compromised by the resentment many of my family members felt towards me, deteriorated further. My relatives justified this on the grounds that I was spoiled by my grandparents and taking advantage of them, and they told me that I should be grateful, because the Lawlor family had taken me in off the street and reared me, even though they did not have to. I justified my own attitude on the grounds that they and their children had everything I had ever wanted – parents to take care of them – while I was all alone.

5

Life Moved On

One of the things that had kept Mam going when I was little was the huge amount of encouragement and positivity she received from her friends in relation to bringing me up. She had never recovered from the loss of Francis, but she had found meaning and hope in her responsibility for me. When I was a toddler and little girl, she was always surrounded by well-wishers telling her what a pretty child I was, and what a wonderful thing she was doing, taking me in and raising me as though I were her daughter, even though she had already raised 12 children of her own. None of her friends ever stopped caring about her, but as the years passed, inevitably life moved on.

When I was small, the anniversary Mass for my parents had always been a huge annual event, and preparing for the Mass and for the refreshments at our house afterwards had kept Mam busy and focused on the here and now, even though it was the anniversary of such a terrible disaster. The love and support that her friends offered her at those times had kept her going throughout my early childhood. Now, with the tragedy and grief less immediate, people were less proactive in offering support.

As I got older, we kept up the tradition of the anniversary Mass (now held at Our Lady of Lourdes Church on Séan MacDermott Street) but the parties in memory of Francis's short and wonderful life had become a thing of the past. I was too big now to be dressed in velvet and passed from one lap to another like a living doll – and I was no longer an endearing, if tragic, toddler with her whole life ahead of her, but a damaged teenager struggling with her mental health, constantly on the verge of dropping out of school, and with no meaningful plans for the future.

Mam continued to feel very close to Francis. In the kitchen, she kept a photograph of him, taken on the day of his passing out with the Irish army; it had been in the front room of the old house. While all the other family photographs on display were glazed, Mam felt that the glass would be yet another barrier between her and her dead son, so Francis's photo was bare. Over the years, it had become warped and stained by the heat and the air-borne grease of the kitchen, and by the time I was really aware of it, it had become quite distorted. That did not matter to Mam, who always positioned herself in her favourite chair so that she was at eye-level with the image all the time. On difficult days, she would sigh loudly as she gazed at Francis.

"God," Mam would say, "please take me in the midst of my sin to my son."

Because Mam cried so often when she was looking at Francis's photograph, one day I moved it to another shelf, reasoning that maybe if she could not see it, she would feel a little better. But as soon as Mam came in with her shopping bags, she dropped them heavily on the floor, her expression leaden.

"Where's my photo?" she asked me. "Put your father back at once on his shelf."

Disturbed by the unusual severity of her tone, I did as I was told.

We knew that a considerable sum of money had been put aside for me when I was older from the compensation fund set up by the government for the victims of the Stardust disaster and their families. This became a problem for my extended family, who could see that raising me was not always easy for my aging grandmother. Some of my relatives were angry that I was going to get money from the government "for nothing", just because my parents had died, while Mam and Grandad, and the rest of the family, had never had anything "handed to them on a plate".

People frequently talked about the money I was going to get: how my life would be different when I got my money; how I would not know myself, because I would be like a millionaire; how I would have to be sure to remember everyone else in the family when I was rich, because they had been there for me all my life and had taken me in off the street when my own mother's family had handed me over.

For me at this time, the prospect of having money when I was older seemed like a distant dream. Most of the time I forgot about it, but every so often, I remembered and would start prattling on to Mam about it.

"I'm gonna get you a big house on the hill of Howth next door to Gaybo," I would tell her (Howth is an up-market suburb of Dublin with gorgeous views of the Irish Sea, and "Gaybo" was Gay Byrne, Ireland's most famous television presenter), "and I'll have three cars… and we'll get ice cream whenever we want! What d'you think of that?"

"That'll be only gorgeous, love," Mam would say, humouring me. "You'll be able to buy a big house out beside your mammy and daddy in Sutton and it'll be a great comfort to them having you around the corner."

Mam thought it would be nice if I lived near the graveyard where my parents were buried, so that I would be able to visit them whenever I wanted.

"Yeah, Mam," I said. "I'll live out beside them. That'll be lovely. Then I'll be able to bring them flowers every day."

Sometimes when the topic of the money came up, someone would mutter about how it was not right that I was going to get it all, when other people were going to so much effort to bring me up and getting nothing for it in return but cheek. Someone else would say that, with all the money coming my way, it was ridiculous that I was getting so much pocket money (£20 a week, which was a lot at the time). Then someone would chime in that I thought I was great, because everyone knew who I was, and that I thought I was a film star and had a big head. Mam would tell them to stop, because it was not my fault that my parents were gone, and that I deserved enough money to give me a good start in life, especially because she and Grandad might well die before they saw me walk up the aisle and start a family of my own. Then, I would need all the help I could get.

"Don't you start on my Lisa," Mam would warn anyone who complained about the money I was going to get. "That poor child breaks my heart every single day – just to look at her and know how much she's lost. She's the only thing keeping me alive."

I was not the only person breaking Mam's heart. Denis and Alison were heroin addicts. The drugs had stolen their ambition, their drive, and even their personalities. Of course, Mam still loved them with all her heart and did her best to help, but they had gone so far down the path of self-destruction that now they were often more like zombies than human beings. They were getting help from the social services, but it was never enough to get them off the drugs long-term. They would go on methadone for a while, only to relapse the first time they had a bad day, or meet a friend with a new bag of gear. They lied to, stole from, and deceived everyone in their lives.

Several of my family members, who took drugs but never seemed to get addicted to the same extent, had become involved in small-time dealing and robbing, and sometimes got in trouble with the law. Every time, all the details of the crime were splashed all over the newspapers, and all the neighbours knew about it. All of this was absolutely devastating for Mam, who never stopped giving them another chance. Mam said that if Francis had been alive, his siblings' addiction would never have been allowed to take hold of them. Because he was so protective of his younger brothers and sisters, he would have made them see sense before it was too late.

"Your daddy would have killed them before seeing them kill themselves," Mam used to say, dramatically.

Often, I came home from school to find my Aunt Alison sitting in the kitchen, completely unaware of who she was and what she was doing, drool from her slack mouth dropping from her lip and onto the kitchen table where Mam prepared all our meals. Mam would be sitting on the other side of the table, just looking at her and crying helplessly, because there did not seem to be anything she could do. It was hard to even recognise Alison sometimes. The attractive young woman she had once been had been replaced by someone who, at times, came home looking like a shell of herself.

Sometimes Alison was so far gone, I would think that she had died. I would push her gently to see if she stayed upright or fell over. Usually, she barely reacted. I was terrified that one night she just would not wake up, and Mam would have lost another of her children.

I knew that Mam would not be able to cope if one of her children died of an overdose; she had never recovered from Francis's death. I had already learned how to rouse Alison and Denis from a drug coma by slapping them around the face. I knew that if they responded, they were probably okay. If the day came when one of them was unable to respond, that would be the time to call the ambulance.

Although she had a boyfriend – a nice guy called Tony, who had his troubles but who loved her dearly and did his best to take care of her – Alison was living at home, and Mam did everything to keep her alive and try to make it easier for her to come off the drugs.

Nothing helped.

I can see now that it probably would have been better for everyone if Alison had been asked to leave – maybe she would have found a way to get back on her feet if she had been out on her own – but Mam just loved all her children so much, she would never have done that to any of them. She just kept right on cleaning up after and cooking for Alison and all the rest of us as though nothing was wrong and it might all just sort itself out one of these days.

I worried that maybe because Mam was giving me so attention, she did not have enough left for the others. I wondered if that meant that their addiction was my fault, or another sorrow that, somehow, I had introduced to the house just by existing.

Alison and Denis were so addicted to heroin, they could not even imagine coming off it. When they got their dole money, they usually blew it all at once; those were the days when I would find poor Alison almost comatose at the kitchen table. The rest of the time, they raised funds for their habit by picking pockets in town or stealing from their family. They never had to worry about where the next meal was coming from, because Mam would have moved heaven and earth to provide for them.

I swore to myself that I would never get involved with drugs, because it looked so awful. I could not understand the attraction; Alison and Denis just looked utterly miserable whenever they were on the gear. I could see how they were prepared to do anything, including hurting the people who loved them most, just to get their hands on money to buy more drugs. It was easy to tell when they had run short, because I would come home from school and find the house completely trashed, with every drawer thrown on the ground, chairs and tables upside down, and even Mam's plaster saints thrown on the ground – chipped and damaged – as a result of the frantic search for funds. Mam would cry as she picked her saints up, brush them off, and put them back in place.

One morning I was getting ready to leave for school when there was a knock on the door. I opened it and found a couple of gardaí standing there.

"Hello, love," one of the men said. "Is there a grown-up in the house we can talk to?"

My heart leapt into my throat because my first thought was that someone had died. However, they had a warrant for Alison's arrest, as she had been caught shoplifting a pair of shoes from Penney's. Alison's excuse was that she had put the shoes under her arm and had been planning to pay for them, but just forgot. She was so far gone most of the time that this could easily have been true. However, the authorities were not buying any of it, and Alison ended up spending about a week in jail.

Life Moved On

I will never forget how all the colour drained from Mam's face as she watched Alison being led away by the guards. Mam had tried offering them money to make the problem go away, but they said that Alison had to answer for herself. Mam was mortified, because all of the neighbours had come out or pushed their net curtains aside to see what was going on. I had to rush forward and catch Mam by the elbow to stop her from falling over.

I led Mam past the altar with all the saints, and into the front room, and she sank into one of the oversized armchairs. She crossed herself and started to say a prayer, but then she began to cry. I just stood there and looked down at her. I wanted to take her pain away, but I did not know how. I told Mam that I was taking the day off school to stay with her, and she did not even protest about me missing my lessons.

Mam just sat in her chair all day, fretting about Alison while I brought her cups of tea and tried to make her feel better. She could not accept that Alison needed professional help, and was in such denial about the situation that she had convinced herself that it was all just a phase that Alison was going through, and that one day she would just snap out of it and be all right. Even now that Alison had been arrested, Mam was sure that she was just about to turn the corner.

Mam's deep faith in God and the saints did not waver, even in the face of the terrible challenges she was dealing with. She went to Mass less often than she had when we lived in Seville Place on Sheriff Street, but she prayed constantly at home, and every Friday she made her way over to John's Lane church on

Thomas Street, on the south side of the city, to pray before the shrine of Saint Rita of Cascia, after picking up her groceries on nearby Meath Street where, she said, the few remaining traditional butchers worth patronising were located.

Saint Rita was an Italian saint, the Patroness of Hopeless Causes, and therefore the perfect saint for my family's needs. The shrine was really beautiful, with a gorgeous stained-glass window and heaps of offerings left by faithful people like Mam. Unlike Mam, they had prayed to Saint Rita for a miracle and their prayers had been answered. Every week, Mam went in to talk to Saint Rita and ask her to intervene with our family, because it seemed that no matter how much Mam loved her many children, and despite all that she did for them, some of them were determined to remain irredeemably lost. I am sure that Mam prayed for me too; I know that she hoped that I would learn how to focus and start to do better at school. I am sure that she was terrified that I would be taken away from her by heroin as well.

Mam and Grandad decided that the best way to keep me safe from the dreaded heroin was to limit the extent to which I was allowed out. I was just beginning to take an interest in boys, but I was given very few opportunities to get to know any. I was occasionally allowed to go to an alcohol-free disco on Griffith Avenue; I remember the sheer embarrassment I felt when I came out with my arm linked with that of a boy of about my own age, only to see my grandfather waiting outside for me.

"Where's your fuckin' coat?" Grandad roared as I shrieked and ran away from him, mortified that my grandfather had come to collect me and had caught me with a boy.

"You were told to wear a warm coat," Grandad persisted. "Look at you out in your slip; you'll catch your death of cold and you're showing that boy everything God gave you. Your grandmother is at home worrying about you; have you no shame?"

Grandad was right about the coat – every time I went anywhere, Mam told me to put on a warm coat so that the cold air would not reach my kidneys. From the age of 13 or so, I had developed a deep hatred of my coat, and while I agreed to wear it and let her button it up to my chin, I used to take it off in the porch, roll it into a ball, and hide it in the corner.

I had plenty of fashionable things to wear, because every week I went into Henry Street and blew all of my pocket money on dresses, blouses, make-up, and cheap perfume. I was often quite generous with my friends, who never had as much pocket money as I did, because I wanted them to like me, and felt that spending money on them and giving them presents was the best way to ensure that they continued wanting to spend time with me. Not wearing my coat when I went out was another way of getting positive attention, because I was developing a pretty figure and I liked to show it off.

Grandad and Mam had always presented a united front, but as Alison and Denis gave themselves over more and more to heroin, they started to differ over how to deal with their children's addiction – and how to make sure that I would not succumb to it, as well. Mam felt that if she was always there for her adult children with three-course meals, prayers, and love, eventually they would see sense, come off the drugs, and stop getting into trouble with the law. Grandad had gone along with this idea for a while, but now he had had enough. He decided that if anyone came back to the house on drugs, he was not going to let them in. Mam felt that if I knew that she was always there for me, and that I was always safe with her, I would not feel tempted to take drugs – and Grandad retorted that this approach had not worked for the others, and that maybe some tough love would be the best way to keep me on the straight and narrow.

While I can only imagine how difficult the situation was for my grandfather, his attitude made everything worse.

While Alison and Denis were often off their heads on drugs, Grandad was just as likely to have seven or eight pints of Guinness under his belt; now that he was only working part-time, he had a lot more time to spend in the pub, and plenty of energy to devote to anger and drinking. Someone would turn up, clearly off their head on drugs, and he would go to the door and start yelling and screaming and threatening them with violence, while Mam screamed back at him and tried to get him to change his mind. Alison and Denis would give as good as they got, shouting back and eventually getting their own way because they were making such a scene in front of the neighbours.

Grandad decided that the problem was that Mam had been too soft with the children all along, that she had spoiled them when they were growing up, and as a result had no moral fibre and were incapable of making good decisions. He further decided that, as I was spoiled too, I was likely to start taking heroin any day now or to do something stupid, like get pregnant before I turned 15. He determined that if Mam was not going to discipline me, then he was the one to do it.

I am the first to admit that I was actually very spoiled by my grandmother – but Grandad felt that the best way to keep me on the straight and narrow was to become immensely strict and even aggressive. From when I reached the age of 14 or so, every single time I stepped out of line, Grandad became verbally abusive and could even be violent at times.

Once I had my hair done in cornrows in Crown Alley in Temple Bar, a fashionable area of the city centre. I came home swishing my hundreds of little plaits from side to side, feeling delighted with myself.

As soon as I stepped into the house, Grandad came charging over to me.

"What have to done to yourself, you little tramp?" he yelled. "You're a fuckin' disgrace with your hair like that! Do you think you're on the fuckin' television?"

I could smell the Guinness fumes on Grandad's breath as he grabbed a fistful of plaits at the back of my head and pulled me down, twisting my head around until I was looking up at him from waist height.

"Get them things out of your fuckin' head now," Grandad said. "I don't know who you think you are."

"Why?" I cried. "I didn't do anything wrong. Loads of girls have their hair like this."

"No granddaughter of mine is going to go around looking like that. We have enough troubles here as it is."

From then on, I could not do anything right so far as Grandad was concerned. Some of his complaints about me were at least partly true. Mam had always given me everything I wanted, and had let me get away with cheekiness and naughty behaviour that I should have been reprimanded for. Now that I was a teenager, I was getting bolder and cheekier. I just wish that Grandad had not decided that violence was the best way to show me how he wanted me to behave.

It has taken me a long time to make sense of how my grandfather behaved towards me at this time, and to process the emotions I still feel when I remember the many times he attacked me and called me horrible names. I know that he was getting old, and that living with a teenage girl, while also dealing with adult children who were addicted to heroin, must have been very difficult for him. I think that he was increasingly aware of the resentment and jealousy some of my aunts and uncles felt towards me, and that he often heard complaints about how I took Mam for granted and thought that I was God's gift. I have some sympathy for the situation he was in, but his violence and abusive behaviour made my life miserable.

Next, Grandad decided that we were spending too much money on the house. When he was still working full-time, the house had been Mam's domain, and he had left her to it. But now that he was at home most of the time, Grandad decided that she had been doing everything wrong. He told us that we were only allowed to turn the heating on when he said so, and he would become enraged if anyone left a light on upstairs.

One winter evening, Grandad came in from the pub and found the heating on.

"Who turned that on?" he said. "I never said you could turn the heating on."

"I did," I said. "We were cold. You don't want us to be cold, do you?"

Grandad's face went red and he came right up to me.

"When you're paying the fuckin' bills, you can turn the heating on," he said. "Don't you dare turn the heating on when I'm not here. I'll decide when it's cold; not you. You're a typical Farrell nuisance: always looking for a handout, like your mother. I'm bleedin' sick of you, around the house all the time. Well, your days of being pandered to are over."

As well as being angry with me for being wasteful, Grandad was still angry with the Farrells over how they had turned up on his doorstep with me, four weeks after my parents died, looking for financial help to bury their mother. Now that Grandad was increasingly angry with me, he raked over the story about the Farrells "selling" me over and over again. Then, when he had drunk a few pints, he would start to remember how he had never liked my mother Maureen and had thought that she was not good enough for Francis, the golden boy, who had sacrificed his own beautiful young life in a desperate, futile attempt to save her.

"You're like your fuckin' mother," he would say to me viciously. "She was a wasteful bitch, too. If she'd lived, they wouldn't be together anymore. I can fuckin' guarantee you that."

Until now, I had always been told by Mam that Maureen and Francis were angels in heaven, who had loved me during their short time as my parents and who were now looking down at me and hearing my prayers.

Usually, when my aunts and uncles mentioned my parents, it was to stress how much they had loved each other, and how happy they had been when I was born. When he had had too much to drink and was annoyed with me, the alternative version that Grandad painted of my parents – of a vain, vacuous, and wasteful woman and a man who did not really love her – was unbearable. I knew that what he was saying was not true and that he was only trying to hurt me – but it did hurt. It hurt terribly. In fact, it still does. I will never understand how Grandad could have spoken like that about his own son and daughter-in-law, whose brief lives had ended so tragically. It was as though a sore had been festering inside him for years, and now something had ruptured it, and it was spewing poison out of his mouth – poison that seeped into every corner of our house, and every corner of my heart.

Outside the home, nobody knew what Grandad could be like with Mam and me on his bad days. They just saw an honest, hard-working man with a great work ethic and gentlemanly ways. If we had complained, they would not have recognised him in our stories of his violence and shouting. I became terrified of

Grandad. At home, I would tiptoe around him, trying not to make him angry and set him off. I felt that I was being blamed for everything that went wrong in the house and that maybe if I had not been born, my parents would not have felt the need for a night off, and might never have gone to the Stardust at all. I often thought about killing myself and bringing the pain to an end.

"Mam," I said once. "Grandad is scaring the hell out of me."

The funny thing is that while I was trying to tell Mam all about what Grandad was saying and doing, I was actually laughing at the same time. I think that I did not want to frighten or upset her, so was trying to tell her the truth in a way that made it sound less important than it was.

"Look," said Mam. "Whatever he says, I don't want you to go telling anyone outside the family. Do you understand that? We'll deal with our troubles ourselves. You don't dare take stories about your grandfather outside this house because you know as well as me that he does be only messin'."

Mam was terribly upset by how Grandad was treating me, but she did not have the energy or courage to confront him. She counselled me to just stay quiet and not to provoke him.

"Lisa, pet," Mam would say. "Don't let this be the hill you die on. It's not worth it. Let it go. He loves you really. You know he doesn't mean it."

For once in her life, Mam actually looked like she might be getting angry with me. I quickly promised that I would never tell anyone outside the family a thing, and I never raised the issue with her again.

The angrier my grandfather got, the worse Alison and Denis's addiction got, and the less Mam was able to cope, the more I wanted to be anywhere but home. I knew that Mam loved me, but she was so sad all the time she did not have the energy to stand up for me anymore.

While I still vaguely hoped that I would grow close to some of my Farrell relatives, I actually had very little contact with that side of my family at this time, apart from the occasional meet-up with my Aunt Marian, who was always good to me. Marian was a quiet woman who did not say much, but she did her best to make me feel welcome, often cooking me a plate of chips with curry sauce when I visited her in her home, or getting me a treat from the local take-away. Marian had three children who were quite close in age to me, but we did not spend enough time together to really become friendly, although they were never anything but kind. I think that it was very difficult for my cousins to get to know me and to develop warm feelings for me, because I had become quite a difficult girl: I was needy and vulnerable and desperately wanted attention and approval from my whole extended family, but then at the same time I could be self-centred, wayward, and prickly, and often pushed away the very people I wanted to love me. I was very anxious and nervous, and felt that whenever anyone expressed a negative thought or feeling about anything, it had something to do with me.

From the age of about 14, I started to raid the drinks cupboard and take whatever I could get my hands on to the park to share with my friends. It was all quite ordinary teenage behaviour – at the start, I never stole enough for us to get seriously drunk and I liked the idea that we were pulling the wool over Grandad's eyes, because he never knew how much drink he had in the liquor cabinet. I never got caught – not until I tried to top up the Pernod bottle with water, and got found out when the liquid inside turned milky-opaque. Grandad was so angry he could have killed me.

Gradually, I started drinking more and more heavily and I bought a baby bottle for my illicit booze. I was a thin little girl who could not handle the drink, and one night at a teenage disco, I got so drunk one of the security men had to bring me home. I was not even able to stand up, so thank goodness he was an honourable man, and not the sort to take advantage of a young girl. Denis opened the door and thanked the man for bringing me home safely. I woke up the next morning with my hair stuck to my face with vomit. Mam felt so sorry for me, I did not really get in trouble, but she handed me the Hoover and told me to give the house a good clean from top to bottom.

"Now," she said, "you won't do that again in a hurry, will you?"

I spent the rest of the day cleaning the house painfully slowly, pausing now and again to rush to the toilet to be sick. I was sure I would never want to have another drop of alcohol as long as I lived.

At this time, I was desperate for positive attention from other young people – much like any other teenager, I suppose. I realised that my status as the Stardust Baby made me a sort of celebrity in the eyes of some of the families around the area, many of whom had friends, relatives, or acquaintances who had died or been injured in the fire. It sounds ridiculous, but that is the way it was. All the girls at school knew that I was the Stardust orphan, and every time I was introduced to someone new, they would say, "This is Lisa – the Stardust Baby. Her mammy and daddy were burned to death in the fire."

Sometimes, people even asked to be introduced to me, and then would stare at me as though I knew some sort of secret, or could provide some sort of insight into what it had been like on that awful night. Much as I hated the fact that everyone knew who I was for such a sad reason, a part of me liked the attention, because I did not feel that I was special in any other way, and it was all I had.

I did not go to Mass with Mam as often as before, but I continued to pray, as she had taught me to do from early childhood. Every night, I said three Hail Marys and three Our Fathers and asked God to keep everyone I loved safe. I still believed that not just God, but also my parents, could hear my words, and that my mum and dad were doing whatever they could in heaven to take care of me.

I was too young to be involved, but all this time, the Keegans and other family members of the Stardust disaster were working hard for justice to be served. Nobody had ever been punished for the grotesque negligence that had led to all those deaths, and even 13 years later, the anger and hurt was still raw. The family that owned the Stardust, the Butterlys, was still rich and successful, still hobnobbing with some of the most powerful people in Dublin, and the families whose children had died were still suffering and waiting for answers.

Mam took me to visit my parents' graves at the cemetery in Sutton now and again, and sometimes I went up to Fairview and took the bus to visit them on my own. On the way there, I would have a sense of expectation, as though I would be able to connect with them, or as though they would communicate with me in some way. Sometimes I brought a packet of King crisps and a bottle of lemonade to share with my mummy and daddy. I would pour the lemonade into the earth and leave the crisps on my dad's grave when I left.

When I stood by my father's grave, I always felt a presence, as though he was looking down on me and sending me his love. But at my mother's, I felt nothing at all, even though I spoke to her in my mind all the time. Only years later would I learn that nobody knows for sure if Maureen's shattered remains were buried here, or those of another dancer, destroyed beyond recognition by the Stardust fire.

6

End of Childhood

Third year in secondary school was the year of the Intermediate Certificate exam. I was dreading it because I was completely sure that I would fail. I had never felt secure or safe in school, and now, with the prospect of the exams and my inevitable failure looming, I just did not want to be there at all. I did what I always did: ran away from my fears and tried not to think about them while making excuses for myself on the grounds that I could not be expected to do better because I was the Stardust Baby.

Although I was embarrassed about how poor my academic performance was, I told the other girls at school I did not care, and that I was never going to have to work anyway, because as the Stardust Baby, I was going to get a huge sum of money from the government as soon as I turned 18. Although I was full of bravado, I was afraid that the other girls were laughing at me behind my back and that they found me pathetic.

Mam's health had taken a serious downturn and she had aged a lot, very suddenly. Because she had been a heavy smoker since she was a young girl, her lungs were extremely compromised. She had now been diagnosed with emphysema, and the specialist had given her inhalers and extra oxygen, which she had to carry with her everywhere she went. This was upsetting for her, because she was used to thinking of herself as a strong woman who could take care of herself as well as everybody else. Despite her new medication, Mam coughed all the time, and the slightest exertion exhausted her. She left the house much less than before, and while she continued to prepare her legendary meals for the family, the work took a lot out of her. I knew that she was worried about what was going to become of me, now that I was about to drop out of school, and I felt awful about causing her so much stress, while also powerless to change anything.

"Lisa, love," Mam would say. "The one thing I want from you right now is for you to focus on your education. Will you try to do that for me? I want to die knowing that you'll be able to take care of yourself. That way I can die happy."

The problem was that Mam was asking me to do the one thing that I felt was beyond me. While the teachers at school stressed the importance of regular attendance and of studying hard, I just did not care anymore, and I had given up on even trying to acquire a decent minimum standard of education. School was a miserable place for me. I was failing everything, and everyone knew it. I felt stupid and was sure that everyone else thought that I was stupid, too. The only time I got any positive attention at school was when someone felt sorry for me because both my parents had died in Ireland's most infamous disaster.

At the same time, with my grandmother's declining health, I was still genuinely terrified that, if I was in school all day, something awful might happen to Mam while I was away, and she would die because I had not been there to summon help. I continued to imagine coming home and finding Mam collapsed on the kitchen floor, or an ambulance or the guards outside wheeling a shrouded figure on a gurney, telling me that if only someone had been there, she would have been all right. If that happened, I thought, Mam's death would be my fault, and not only would I be alone in the world, but everyone would blame me for causing her so much trouble and heartache ever since she took me in as a baby.

As well as Mam's poor health, there was so much chaos in the family now, I never knew what I was going to come home to. The one place where I should have been able to feel safe seemed anything but. There was always a crisis brewing or underway. When I was not fretting about coming home from school to find Mam dead, I was panicking that it would be my aunt or uncle, dead from an overdose after so many near-misses.

Poor Alison, who lived at home, was not well at all – she existed from one hit of heroin to the next and while she was her former warm and charming self some of the time, at others she was completely unrecognisable. The heroin was transforming her appearance too – Alison's teeth had started to fall out, and her cheekbones had taken on that sharp look that is so characteristic of anyone who has a long history of taking the drug.

I often lay awake at night, worrying that Alison might die in her sleep. Alison and I did have some good times, even when she was really struggling, and she was one of the people I loved most, and a real ally. At this time in my life, she was not just my aunt, but one of my best friends, and even something of a mother figure to me. On her good days, she and I would get dressed up together, put on some red lipstick, and go out. Alison and her boyfriend Tony often took me with them when they hit the town, and they were always extremely kind and generous. On those evenings, I could still see her as the vibrant young woman she really was underneath her drug-addled persona.

Denis was also completely immersed in his addiction. His lively personality and quick humour had been stolen by the drug, and now he frequently turned up at the door, almost unrecognisable as his former self, whining for hand-outs and threatening to turn violent if he did not get his way. Grandad would try to stick to his word and make him go away, but eventually he made so much fuss that the neighbours would start to look out their windows to see what was going on, and he would relent and let Denis in.

At this time, a friend of the family's had been caught dealing drugs by the authorities, and was serving a five-year sentence in Mountjoy jail. Alison and Denis felt sorry for their friend, who was stressed and upset at the prospect of spending so much time behind bars. They told me that the only thing that would cheer him up was some marijuana that he would be able to enjoy and to share with his friends on the inside. Neither of them could take it to him, so they persuaded me to go up to the jail on visiting day pretending to be the prisoner's daughter, with a little packet of marijuana hidden inside my cheek. They explained how I could quickly and carefully pass the drugs to him when I kissed him hello, and we practised a few times at home until I knew what I was doing.

I was absolutely terrified when the huge gate swung closed behind me with a bang. When I kissed "Daddy", I passed the packet to the prisoner who hid it under his tongue and told me that I was a good girl. I was pleased that he was happy with me, but scared of getting caught by the prison guards; I felt like some sort of gangster's moll and the whole time I was there, I imagined getting caught and thrown before the courts.

Looking back now, I am horrified by what my Alison and Denis expected me to do. They were the adults in my life, and they should have been watching out for me rather than getting me involved in their illegal schemes.

With so much chaos going on all around me, I decided that as I was doing so poorly at school anyway, it made more sense for me to stay at home to take care of Mam and to make sure that she was not getting hassled.

Mam's poor health and the difficulties she was having with some of her adult children was just the excuse that I was looking for. So, most days, I simply did not go to school, and increasingly Mam just did not have the energy to make me go. She used the little fight she had left in her to try to take care of the others, hoping that she could get them off the drugs through the sheer force of her love, and to keep things as calm as possible within the four walls of our broken home. Nobody could ever accuse her of not doing everything within her power to help those she loved. On several occasions, Mam was so unwell that the doctor wanted her to be admitted to hospital so that she could receive specialist treatment. She always refused to go, saying that she would prefer to suffer at home and know that her family had her there to take care of them.

I knew that Mam did not want to abandon me to my grandfather's increasingly erratic tempers and my aunt and uncle's struggles with addiction.

"You've lost enough in your short life, pet," she said. "I wouldn't want to go off to the hospital and leave you on your own."

I was grateful to Mam for caring about me so much, but at the same time I felt awful, because I thought I was denying her the medical attention she so badly needed.

Grandad was furious with me for staying off school so much of the time. The anger, shame, and disappointment he felt about some of his children succumbing to drugs and crime was often taken out on me. Grandad was in his late sixties now, and must have felt that, instead of enjoying a peaceful retirement, he was going to spend his declining years surrounded by constant noise, violence and chaos.

While I have more understanding now of Grandad's point of view, I still do not feel that he handled my truanting very well; he made me the scapegoat for all the anger he felt towards so many members of the family, just because I was there, and I was an easy target. Whenever Grandad found out that I had taken yet another day off school he would start roaring and screaming at me, and telling Mam that she was a fool to let me get away with so much.

"You have that child destroyed with all your spoiling," Grandad said. "You've indulged her and let her get away with everything, and now look at her – she's bleedin' useless. She hasn't the sense she was born with, and she's going to end up a fuckin' junkie like the other useless lumps you reared. Well, I hope you're both very proud of yourselves, because the Lawlor name has been dragged through the mud and I can't so much as hold my head up high around here anymore. I don't feel like I can walk the fuckin' streets without feeling ashamed."

Then Mam would start to cry because, even though she had always done her absolute best with me, to make sure that I was happy and did not miss out on the good things in life despite my parents being dead, she was afraid that Grandad was right and that I was wasting my life. She had felt so proud of me and of herself, for raising me. Now, Grandad was telling her that she had failed at the one thing she had always been good at – taking care of her loved ones. He was challenging her whole identity and the single source of her pride and self-esteem as a traditional wife and mother.

I could not bear to listen to Grandad. His words hurt me incalculably, partly because of the anger with which they were spoken, but also because I was afraid that he was right about me, and that – at 15 – I was already a loser who would never amount to anything and would only ever bring shame down on the family. Whenever he got started with his criticisms, as soon as I got a chance, I would creep up to my room and sit in front of my dressing-table, spraying perfume on myself and trying on all my lipsticks, looking at myself in the mirror and making myself as pretty as possible, because at least that was something I could do, even if I was failing at everything else.

I did try to make myself useful all those days I stayed at home instead of going to school. Mam struggled to breathe, so I opened all the windows and doors, and cleaned the house from top to bottom so that there was no dust to cause her problems with her lungs. I did everything that Mam was unable to do anymore – all the carrying and lifting that I could manage, and even some of the cooking, although I would never be as good at it as her. Mam appreciated my work, but she still wished that I was going to school instead.

"Lisa, love," Mam would say, "what's going to happen to you if you don't get your exams? What are you going to do with your life? Can you not try to be more like your cousin Mary? She's a grand girl and she'll go on to have a good job. She'll be able to take care of herself and will never have to rely on any man. You have my heart scalded. I have the ears talked off Saint Anthony trying to get you through school. Jesus, there's no prayers will work for you! Will you not go back? Make the effort?"

"I'll be grand," I would tell her. "I'll go and learn how to be a hairdresser. I don't need to go to school for that. Hairdressers can earn very good money, you know."

I never had any intention of learning to be a hairdresser. I knew that I was going to get my compensation money from the state as soon as I turned 18, and I thought that I would be set up for life and would never need to work at all.

Mam was too tired to fight back. She probably knew that a hairdressing apprenticeship was never going to happen, but she went along with the idea anyway and if anyone asked her what my plans were, that is what she told them: "My Lisa is going to be a hairdresser. She's always been a great one for the style!"

I wish now that nobody had ever told me as a child that there was money coming my way; whatever little ambition I might have had had been completely obliterated by the knowledge that I was going to get a large lump sum to pay me back for the loss of my parents. With my teenage naivety, I thought that the money would be enough to take care of me for the rest of my life and that I did not need to pass any exams, as my compensation money was there for me instead of a career.

At this time, I was very friendly with Maria and Nikki McConnell, two young girls who lived in the area. We used to have a good laugh together and share some illicit cans in the local park. I also met my first real boyfriend, Brian – a cousin of Maria and Nikki's – around this time. Brian was a lovely boy — tall and handsome, and very sweet. Brian and I never did more than hold hands and hug each other, but Mam was terrified that I would get pregnant at 15, and ruin my life completely. Nonetheless, she let me meet up with him, because she knew that there was no way to stop me.

Brian attended a big comprehensive school called Mount Temple. I used to walk up to meet him after school, and we would stroll home together, holding hands. Brian was proud of being seen with me because he thought I was a stylish dresser — despite being disappointed in me, Mam still gave me everything I wanted, and I had plenty of money to spend on clothes and make-up.

I turned up at the end of the school year to sit my Intermediate Certificate exam, because Mam said I had to, but I had missed so much school by then I did not even understand half the questions on the paper, let alone know how to answer them. I was mortified, and knowing it was all my own fault did not help in the least.

Around then, Brian and I split up — not for any real reason that I can remember, but just because it was an ordinary teenage relationship that had run its course. Anyway, I thought that I might prefer to go out with an older man who would be able to take care of me. While the other girls I knew were always squealing about some lad they had met in a disco and how gorgeous he was, or hanging up posters of good-looking pop stars in their bedrooms, I often found myself looking at my friends' dads and thinking that they were lovely. I did not actually imagine going out with them, but I did think that it would be wonderful to have a kind older man to come home to, who would put his arms around me, set me on his lap, and tell me that he loved me just the way I was, and that I was perfect and did not need to change in any way. My dream man did not wear fashionable jeans and tops, but a jacket and formal trousers. My dream man looked like a loving father who would always be there to take care of me and tell me that everything was all right.

When we had moved to Marino, my aunts and uncles who lived in the area had promised Mam that they would help her to bring me up. I am sure that they were all very concerned about her health and whether she had enough energy to deal with an active teenage girl. Those who were not on drugs, and were just working hard and raising their families, must have also been extremely distressed about the fact that several of their siblings were addicts and criminals. I believe that initially they meant well and only wanted the best for me, but as time passed, from my perspective it seemed as though they had all turned against me.

When it was clear that I was planning to drop out of school as soon as the Intermediate Certificate was over, Mam and I both heard a lot of choice words about the sort of young woman I was growing into. Several of my aunts and uncles started telling Mam that she had wrecked my life by spoiling me, and that it was her fault that I was dropping out of school. They told her that if she had taken a more severe approach with me, I would be more obedient and less reckless. They suggested that perhaps I was at risk of going down the same path as poor Alison and that it was only a matter of time before I was taking drugs and – in all likelihood – walking the streets to fund my addiction.

In retrospect, I can see that my aunts and uncles had a point in some ways, because Mam did spoil me, and while she did so out of love, her approach to raising me was not always in my best interests. The problem was that this message was not delivered in a kind, loving, and constructive manner, but in a harsh and pointed way that broke Mam's big heart. She had always done her best. She had filled my childhood with love, kindness, and affection, and while she lavished me with attention and gifts, and never said no, it had all been done with the best of intentions. In the absence of the professional psychological help she really needed, Mam's only therapy had been trying to make me as happy as I could possibly be.

For me, as a 15-year-old girl with severe problems around anxiety and self-esteem, all I picked up from my relatives' attempts to intervene with Mam was that they did not like me and thought that I had already destroyed my life before it had even begun. This did not encourage me to try to do better, but rather solidified both my tendency to rebel and my view that I was already damaged goods and would never amount to anything on my own.

I had long felt that, somehow, everything that went wrong for my family was my fault. I knew that my extended family were worried that I was too much work for Mam, and this meant that I was responsible for her bad health. I knew that my family's struggles with heroin had begun after I came to live with Mam and Grandad, and thought that, without me, maybe everything would have been okay. In my darkest moments, I wondered if maybe I had always been a problem – if I had been such an awful baby that my parents had wanted to get away from me, which is why they went to the Stardust that night, and why they never came home. Perhaps, I thought, the whole world would have been a better place if I had never been born. Perhaps I had been the catalyst that had sent this ordinary Dublin family spiralling towards disaster.

At this time, Grandad seemed to feel awkward about having a teenage girl in the house. When I was little, he was always at work, and left all the childcare to Mam. Now that I was big, he was home a lot more, and took more interest in me, albeit not in a way that I appreciated. I was used to him being angry with me, but this was something different.

Sometimes Grandad came into my room and looked at me when he thought I was asleep.

Sometimes I heard the floorboards creaking on the landing when I was having a shower, and once when I peeped through the keyhole to see who was there, all I saw was Grandad's bloodshot eye looking in at me. I screamed and covered myself with a towel.

"Go away! Go away!" I shouted.

"What are you bleedin' screamin' for?" Grandad shouted. "Nobody's after touchin' you. I was just makin' sure you were all right."

"Go away!" I shrieked again. I was mortified at the thought of having been seen naked by my grandfather. "Just go away!"

Grandad went away, muttering to himself about how I was making a fuss about nothing, but I was confused and upset as to why he would want to spy on me in the bathroom.

I told a couple of my Lawlor aunts about what had happened. One told me to let it go, as Grandad liked a drink and didn't know what he was doing half the time. The other said that he was getting old and a bit confused and that I needed to be more understanding of his little ways, which were harmless and did not mean anything. I also confided in my Aunt Kathleen, on the Farrell side. I was very upset when I told Kathleen, and she commiserated with me, saying that Grandad had always had a reputation for being difficult with girls and women. Alison, who also had to deal with Grandad's strange behaviour at home, took it all in her stride.

"Don't be mindin' him," Alison said with a laugh. "Sure, he's a harmless aul' fella. I'll put him in his place."

Alison accompanied Grandad to collect his pension every Friday, after which they went to the pub together, giving her the opportunity to skim some of the money off to help pay for her drug habit. She was never going to stand up to Grandad, because it just was not in her interest to do so.

One of my cousins privately told me that she had always been warned as a child not to leave the little ones alone with Grandad, and now she suggested that maybe this was why; that maybe everyone knew that his behaviour could be inappropriate at times.

I believe that everyone knew that Grandad's behaviour had started to change because he was not the same man he had been when he was younger, but they were not ready to accept that he might need some help. I hated it so much when Grandad peeped at me or came into my room when I was sleeping that every time the floorboards on the landing creaked, I would panic. If I was in bed, I would roll myself into a ball and tuck my head down, with the idea that I would be safer if I made myself as small as possible. Eventually, either Grandad would go away or I would fall asleep, still in a state of panic.

As well as the peeping, Grandad seemed to be angry with me all the time. He called me "the nuisance". I would hear him saying to Mam, "Is the nuisance here?" I dreaded when he came into a room in case my presence would annoy him in some way. Mam would start crying, and I would feel that I really was a nuisance, because I seemed to bring out negative emotions in everyone, even Mam, who truly loved me.

One evening, Grandad stood at the door of my room, glared at me, and said,

"You're nothing but a fuckin' nuisance like your cunt of a mother, gone before you!"

"Shut up!" I screamed. "Don't you dare say things like that about her! My mother is an angel in heaven and you're nothing but a drunken old man!"

Grandad walked through the door and over towards me.

"No, I won't shut up," he said in a menacing tone, wafting Guinness fumes in my direction with every word he spoke. "We do everything for you and all you are is a nuisance who doesn't contribute a thing. You're every fuckin' stamp of Maureen fuckin' Farrell, and she took away our son and destroyed him. If it wasn't for her, he'd be alive today. You're lucky we took you in off the street when nobody wanted you; not even that woman's useless family."

Why does he keep doing this? I wondered. *What's so fuckin' bad about me that he thinks I deserve it?*

Mam was so worried about me and my future that she listened carefully whenever any of my aunts and uncles criticised the way she had raised me. She decided that if my problems were the result of her spoiling me, then she would try a different approach. Almost overnight, my pocket money was decreased and, for the first time in my life, Mam started to say "no" to my endless requests. I could hardly believe what was happening.

"Well, now, Lisa," my aunties said to me, with a certain air of triumph. "Things are going to start changing around here for you. Your days of being spoiled are over. What do you think about that, then?"

"I don't care," I would say defiantly. "I'll be gettin' my Stardust money soon, loads of it, and then I won't need anything. I'll be rich."

"Don't be cheeky now, love," Mam said. "You know we all want the best for you, and we all have your interests at heart. You know, you could have been brought up by another family, but we couldn't bear to let you go, we loved you so much."

"What are you talkin' about?" I asked. "What other family? Do you mean the Farrells?"

"The Farrells? No, sure they never wanted you after Elizabeth died; didn't they sell you to us on my very own doorstep? No; there was a dentist in Howth wanted to adopt you and give you a home. He got in touch with us and everything, but I said, 'Nobody is going to take my Lisa away. She belongs right here with me.' I knew that it was only right for you to stay with your own family. I needed you, Lisa. You gave me a reason for living when your father was taken away."

I could not believe what I was hearing. So I could have been a dentist's daughter? A wealthy, educated family had wanted me? I imagined myself living in a big, comfortable house in Howth, one of the fanciest suburbs in Dublin. I would have attended a posh school. Nobody would have asked me to bring marijuana up to a friend in Mountjoy jail. I would never have had to deal with my relatives scream- ing and roaring and tearing the house apart because they needed money for their next heroin fix. I would have been a completely different person. I wondered if I would have been a better one.

In the privacy of my room, I threw myself face-down on my bed and I cried and cried. All my life, people had given me things because they felt sorry for me and wanted to show me that they loved me. When I was little, it had been lollipops, dolls, pretty dresses, and all the treats I wanted. When I got older, it was money to buy clothes, cosmetics, and endless bottles of perfume. I had picked up the idea that if you loved someone, you gave them presents and money. Now I thought that because Mam was not giving me as much as before, she did not love me anymore. I already knew that Grandad did not love me, or even like me, and perhaps never had. I could not bear the idea that Mam had stopped loving me, too.

I decided that I had had enough.

I ran a bath and went to fetch a little penknife that I kept in my room. It was very sharp, and I always had to be careful not to nick myself with the blade when I used it. I remember sitting on the edge of the bath, looking down at my thin white arms and gathering the courage to cut into my wrists until they were bleeding. I cut into my flesh as hard as I could. I thought about getting in the bath and watching the water gradually turn red, imagining what the release would feel like as I faded away into the peace of oblivion. Surely it would be better for me – better for everyone this way…

I'll be with my Ma and Da soon, I thought. *It'll take half an hour at most, and then we'll all be together in heaven. It'll take 10 minutes to bleed, 10 minutes to pass out, and 10 minutes to die. I won't feel anything, and then all my pain will be over.*

I started to imagine myself lying in the red water, with my hair all spread out behind me, pale and still. I thought about how sorry everyone would be that I had died, and how they would finally realise that they had been treating me unfairly.

At the last minute, before stepping into the water, I panicked, realising that I did not really want to die. I just wanted the pain to stop. I just wanted my life to be different. I wanted Grandad to feel sorry for me, realise how badly he had been treating me, and change his ways. I wanted him to see what he was doing to me, and tell me that he loved me after all. I wanted Mam to love me and indulge me, as she always had.

I got some bandages and wrapped up my wrists – the wounds were not very deep, although I do still have the scars today, probably because I didn't go to the doctor for the stitches I needed. I sat on the edge of my bed until Alison came home, and then I told her what I had done.

"Kill yourself because you're upset with Da?" said Alison, scoffing. "He isn't fuckin' worth it. Don't give him any reason to give out. Just go along with it. Come on, Lisa. You're better than he is. You're worth more than that. Sure, he says all the same things to me, and I just tell him to fuck off!"

Alison knew exactly what I was talking about when I complained about Grandad. The difference was that she was so deeply addicted, he was the least of her troubles. Half the time she could not even hear what he was saying.

"I'm just so fed up with him, Alison," I said. "It's not right, the way he goes on. I just wish there were something I could do to make him stop."

"Don't let him get to you, pet," Alison said. "Don't be mindin' him. Do you want me to stay with you? He won't dare bother you if I'm there too – and if he does, we'll take him on together."

Alison and I shared my bed for a while. Feeling her warm body, and hearing her breathe beside me, made it all seem much better. I believe that my parents were looking down on me that night and that they sent Alison to take care of me. They knew that I had my whole life ahead of me, and they did not want me to give up.

While I continued to cut myself sometimes to relieve the feelings of stress I experienced, I never again felt tempted to hurt myself so badly that I could die. I was careful to cut myself in places that would be easy to hide – above my wrists and at the top of my legs. I would start to experience a sense of relief the moment the first dots of red blood welled up on my pale skin. That sense of relief became addictive and compelling, and would drive me to cut myself again the next time I was stressed or upset. I can still see the scars today, silvery scratches that relate the story of my pain. The worst scars, however, are in my mind.

My aunts were very critical of me at this time, but I do believe that they were trying to help in their own way. They were right in saying that Mam had been too lenient with me over the years, and that ultimately it was not doing me any good. The problem was that Mam should have made changes when I was little, before I internalised the lesson that when you loved someone, it meant you gave them things. While people had pointed out how spoiled I was back then, nobody had ever really explained to Mam that I needed to learn how to stand on my own two feet, and that the way she showed her love for me did not always help.

I think that the extended family felt very ambivalent towards me then. They were worried about Mam, and could see how my rebellious streak was causing her a lot of stress and anxiety at a time in her life when she should have been relaxing and focusing on herself. They cared about me – or at least some of them did – but they also resented me because of the pressure my very existence put on Mam, because I appeared wilful and ungrateful, and because I was going to get a huge cheque from the government as soon as I turned 18, without having done anything to earn it.

On holiday in the Canaries with my aunt, we were out at a restaurant one day when I noticed another Irish woman staring at me.

"I'm sorry, love," the woman said, coming over to me. "But I know your face. How do I know you?"

"Where are you from?" I asked her.

"Cabra," she said. She could tell that I was from Dublin because of my accent, so she did not have to explain to me where Cabra is.

"Cabra is where my mother grew up," I said. "Her family still lives there."

"Oh, that might be it," she replied. "What's your mammy's name? Maybe I went to school with her."

"Maureen Farrell," I said.

The woman burst into tears.

"I don't believe it," she said. "Are you Maureen Farrell's baby girl? The Stardust Baby? Come here 'til I give you a hug. I used to be a great friend of Maureen's. We used to hang around together all the time when we were kids. God, you're the living image of her. The very spit."

I started to move towards the woman for the hug she wanted, but my aunt put her hand on my arm in warning.

"All right, Lisa," she said. "That's enough of that. Stop making a show of yourself."

My aunt nodded curtly at the woman to dismiss her and moved me on. I think everyone was sick and tired of me getting so much attention and that she thought that it was bad for me. It did not seem to occur to anyone that this was the sort of attention I would have done anything to live without, as it seemed to me that people only liked me because my parents were dead.

After the holiday, the Intermediate Certificate results came out. My cousin Mary rang in for hers, and as predicted, she had done very well. She had passed everything, and had got honours in several subjects. Her family was rightly very proud of her achievements. I had failed all but three subjects. I had even failed foundation maths, which everyone knew was only for dummies. I had already decided that I was not going back to school – but at this point, the school probably would not have wanted me anyway. When people asked me how I felt about the results, I just tossed my head and said I didn't give a shit. It was not true; I would have done anything to be half as clever as Mary, but I thought that if I admitted how bad I felt about my performance, I would just get told that it was my own fault for not studying – which was of course the case, because my anxiety took up all of my mental and emotional energy.

Alison came home one day with some big news: she and her boyfriend Tony were having a baby.

"For the love of God, Alison," Mam said, sitting down heavily to process this information. "You can't even take care of yourself; how are you going to take care of a baby? You're not well, love."

"I'll be fine," Alison said. "I'll take care of it. I'll be better when the baby is here; I'm sure of it."

But Alison was still on heroin, and even though she swore to everyone that she was going to stop, she kept on taking drugs the whole way through her pregnancy. She had help from the health service, which provided her with alternative drugs to keep her off the heroin, but so far as we could see, the prescription medication was almost as bad as the stuff Alison bought on the street. The whole family was desperately worried that her drug-taking was going to affect the baby. Mam spent the whole pregnancy praying to God, Mary, and all the saints on behalf of Alison and her child, asking them to watch over her and make sure that the baby was all right.

Despite her troubles, Alison's belly grew, she blossomed, and after nine months, she gave birth to a beautiful, healthy baby girl who she named Emma.

"She's gorgeous, Alo," said Mam. "A real gift from God."

I could see that Mam already loved Emma, as she loved all babies – but we could all see that she was getting older and frailer and was going to be in no way able to help Alison to raise her. Taking care of me had already worn her out and she had very little left to give. Increasingly, I had to take care of Mam, rather than vice versa. I was happy to do this, because I loved her so much, and because I felt that it justified my decision to leave school. Having Emma at home – this perfect, squeezable baby, who needed so much care and love – helped me to feel useful and in charge at a time when I really needed it.

*　*　*

I had often asked Mam why my parents were not buried together, but in separate graves, side by side. For years, she fobbed me off with vague explanations, but eventually, when I was 16, she explained that my mother's injuries had been so extensive, it had taken some time to identify her, and that she had been buried after Francis as a result. When she said that, I felt a tentative blossom of joy begin to flower in my heart.

"Are you sayin' they're not even sure it's her?" I asked. "Like, it could be someone else's bones in there beside my dad's? Anyone's?"

"Well, yeah," said Mam. "They think it's her, but they can't be 100 per cent certain. That fire was awful, and there wasn't very much of her left. I'm sorry, Lee."

"But this is *great!*" I said. "This is really good news! Do you not see what this means, Mam? She might not be dead at all. She might just have got confused and run off. Maybe she's in England, or still in hospital somewhere, and one day she'll realise who she is and come back to me!"

"Ah, Lee." Mam said. "Ah, love…"

Mam burst into tears. She told me no, that my mother was definitely dead and gone, and that there was absolutely no hope of her ever coming back. That she would never have run off on me because she doted on me so much.

I accepted this on one level, because I knew that Mam would never lie to me – but a part of me kept hoping that maybe my mother did run off and might come home one day. I wondered if the strangely disconnected feeling I always experienced at my mother's grave, as compared to my father's, was because she was not there at all. Back at the house, I took out my penknife and slashed at my legs until the pressure building up in my head eased somewhat and I felt a little better.

Even now, there are moments when I still indulge in this fantasy, and think about how wonderful it will be when I feel my mother's loving arms around me and hear her whisper to me that she never meant to leave. That it was all a horrible mistake. That she was just waiting for the right moment to come back into my life.

7

Almost a Grown-up

I spent over a year at home doing the housework and helping to take care of baby Emma. Alison had managed to pull herself together enough to take care of her baby – she was a great mother and she loved Emma to pieces – but she was unable to come off the drugs completely. A clinic provided her with methadone and, while she slipped and took street drugs now and again, most of the time she managed to stay on an even keel. Mam and I helped Alison as much as we could, because we knew that she was really doing her best and needed our support.

I loved Emma, and really enjoyed helping Alison to take care of her: washing her, changing her, and putting on her little dresses. Sometimes Alison and I would take Emma out when we went for something to eat or for a few drinks; everyone would want to come and look at her because she was such a pretty, placid little thing. Emma was like a living doll for me. I loved to pick her up and squeeze her soft little body, dreaming of the day that I would have a gorgeous baby of my own to mother and love.

When she was a little bigger, I brought Emma into town in her pram and wheeled her around the shops, prattling away to her about the pretty dresses and the other things that I liked to look at. I wanted everyone to know that I treasured Emma, so I kept both her and her pram spotless, washing every stain and clearing away every crumb. I remembered the stories I had heard about Maureen, my mum, and how she had always kept me looking perfect as a baby. I tried to be like her.

Although many people endeavoured to encourage me to do something more ambitious with my life, I did not bother trying to find a real job, because I knew that I was going to get my compensation money as soon as I turned 18. While I was happy when I was taking care of Emma, beneath it all I was really quite fed up and disappointed with life, and with myself, and I just lived for the day when my money would turn everything around and I could buy myself the pretty things that I hoped would boost my self-esteem.

Mam was still sick, and I was not getting on well with several of my aunts and uncles, who felt that I should either go back to school and get some qualifications or go out to work and make some money to contribute to the household. They all said that they only had my interests at heart, and I believe that most of them did, but they could be very harsh in their criticisms of me, and I didn't take it very well or respond very productively.

I do not know to what extent my aunties and uncles, with the exception of Alison who lived at home, were aware of some of the troubling aspects of my grandfather's behaviour, which had continued to escalate. When I was in my late teens, Grandad started using a lot of inappropriate language around me, much more than before, and behaving in an embarrassing manner around my friends. He was not the man I had known as a child and seemed not to be able to control his own mind. He often vocalised whatever he was thinking, without pausing to wonder if it was appropriate. I had a pal at the time who was a good-looking girl with a big bust. After visiting me at home a few times, she said that she hoped I wasn't offended, but that she didn't want to come to my house anymore, because she didn't like the way Grandad stared at her breasts and swatted her on the bottom when she walked by.

Sometimes Grandad told me that he came into my room at night to make sure I was all right. I went into a pharmacy and bought some ear plugs so that I would be able to sleep through the night without waking up when he came into my room. I didn't want to challenge him, because the minute I opened my eyes it became real and I didn't understand what he was doing there or why he felt this was a good idea. I preferred to keep my eyes tightly closed and I certainly did not want to upset Mam.

My self-harming escalated; I found a sense of relief when I cut myself, as though some of the pressure and tension I felt inside was leaving my body with the blood that came from my wounds. I was careful to hide my cutting from others; it felt private to me, and I didn't want anyone to know about it. Only Alison knew what I was doing, and she did her best to support me and help me to stop.

Grandad was getting older now, and I have wondered, looking back, if his uninhibited behaviour at this time was the start of some sort of dementia. That would explain his loss of control over his baser instincts and the ebbing away of the protective instinct that he had shown towards me when I was little. I really do not know what came over him. It may not have been intentional, but for me it was devastating and very damaging.

I never told Mam about my fears because I just could not hurt her, and because I knew that, despite everything, Grandad really did love his wife and his family. The last thing I wanted was to come between the two of them at a time when they should have been relaxing and enjoying their golden years together. It was easier just to plug my ears; I rarely acted out as a result of Grandad's behaviour, but rather chose to ignore it.

An exception to this general rule came one day when I confronted Grandad about what he had been doing. We were downstairs in the hall when I lashed out.

"I'm bloody well sick of it!" I shouted. "I know I'm only 16, but I still deserve some respect. I'm a human being! It's not right for you to be talking to me the way you do. It's fuckin' disgusting."

"You do as you're told while you're under my roof!" he retorted. "I'm payin' the bills around here, not you. That means that I'm the one who gets to call the shots, not an ignorant little fuck like you. I'm the captain of this ship, so you can shut the fuck up."

"That doesn't mean I have to put up with all of your shit!" I said. "It's not fair! I never asked to be born or to live with you."

Grandad went red in the face. He came over to me and gave me a hard shove, pushing me against the wall. Then he slapped me in the face. I was so startled, I immediately lashed out and slapped him back across the face, equally hard. While he stood there in shock with a big red handprint on the side of his face — I don't think that he had ever expected me to stand up for myself — I ran out the hall door and made my way through the dark to my auntie's house nearby. As I ran out of the garden, I could hear Grandad beginning to roar and ordering me to come back so that he could finish talking to me.

My auntie and uncle and a friend of theirs were sitting together drinking tea and chatting when I burst in the door, full of indignation.

"What are you so upset about?" someone asked. "Did you see a ghost or something?"

"I'm after slappin' Grandad!" I said. "So I had to get out of there before he went ballistic altogether. I'm not going back until he's had some time to calm the fuck down. That fuckin' aul' fella will be the death of me."

They all just looked at me without making any comment at all. Someone asked me if I wanted a cup of tea and got up to put on the kettle. Nobody seemed curious about why I had slapped my grandfather. Perhaps, I thought, they had a very good idea of what was going on and they did not want to hear it out loud. Maybe they thought I deserved it. Or maybe they didn't realise things had got as serious as they had.

Mam was always my protector, but the general chaos in the family was beginning to damage even our relationship. I felt so lonely and ignored that even Mam's great love for me did not seem to be enough. One day, I came home to find Alison wearing my clothes. I was outraged, and demanded that she give them back. Alison was up to her eyeballs in heroin that day, and she just looked at me blearily and said nothing.

"You leave my Alison alone," said Mam. "She has a headache. She's not well, and she needs to lie down, not listen to you givin' out."

"She has no bleedin' headache!" I said. "Don't make me laugh! She's on the fuckin' gear, as usual. And I want my clothes back."

"No, Lisa..." Mam started to say.

I still cannot believe what happened next. I actually slapped Mam on the face. I stood there and stared in horror as she put her hand to her reddening cheek and looked at me in shock.

"Jesus, Mam, I'm sorry," I said immediately. "I didn't mean it."

"Just get out," said Mam, who was close to tears. "You're not in your right mind."

I left and did not return for a number of hours. We did not talk about this incident again for several days, but a week later, Mam called me downstairs from my room. She told me to kneel on a

Bible and to hold another Bible in my hand. I did what she said, and then Mam balanced a third Bible on top of my head.

"Now," said Mam. "Swear to me on the Bible you'll never raise your hand against me in anger again."

"Oh God, I swear," I said. "I'm so sorry, Mam, and I swear to God, the angels, and on my parents' grave that I'll never do something like that again. Not as long as I live."

"I believe you, pet," said Mam. "Now get up and we'll say no more about it."

Mam took the Bible off my head, and I stood up and hugged her tightly, relieved and grateful for having been forgiven for the awful thing that I had done.

A few weeks later, I was at home when I heard noises from Alison's bedroom. I went in, and found Alison and Denis sitting on the edge of the bed. There was a thick, sweet smell of toffee in the air.

"What's that smell?" I asked, sniffing.

Of course, I knew what it was. The whole neighbourhood was riddled with heroin use, and it seemed as though half the people in my life were on it. For years, seeing how it stole their personalities and their lives, I had been completely repulsed by it. But by now it seemed almost inevitable that I would start taking it too. I was curious to learn just what was so wonderful about heroin that so many of the people I knew were prepared to do almost anything to get it.

Denis laughed. "This the best painkiller in the world," he said. "Do you want some?"

"Give us a bit of that, then," I said. "My stomach is killing me. It's my period. The cramps have me driven mad. I suppose that's why they call it 'the curse'."

"This'll sort you out, then," said Alison. "This is the best sort of painkiller for cramps."

Alison and Denis exchanged nervous smiles. Alison moved up so that I could sit beside them on the edge of the bed, and Denis handed me a silvery "tooter" – a sort of metal straw made of rolled-up tin foil – and told me to put it in my mouth.

He showed me how to light a small piece of heroin in a cradle of tin foil underneath, to watch carefully until it started to melt, and then see the oil roll down the crease in the foil before inhaling the smoke. I tried to do what Denis said.

"Hold on, you're not doin' it right," said Denis. "It's burnin' up; that's how you waste it. Hold it down towards you…"

I did as Denis instructed and could taste the sweet toffee smell at the back of my throat as I inhaled the smoke. I sat on the side of the bed and looked around. Alison and Denis disappeared from my field of vision and the whole room retreated into darkness.

What the fuck is goin' on? I thought. *Is it supposed to be like this?*

Somehow, I managed to stagger out of the room and head upstairs to my own bedroom. I flopped down heavily onto the bed, banging my head hard against the wooden headboard. I could hear Denis and Alison's heavy footsteps on the stairs as they ran after me. I remember lying there moaning, listening to my own voice as though it was coming from somewhere outside my body. Within minutes, I was vomiting uncontrollably. I sat up and projectile-vomited to the end of the bed. Then I collapsed back down again, still vomiting. Now I was barely able to turn my head to the side to do it. Vomit was spewing out of me, all over the pretty floral sheets and pillowcases, and soaking into my long hair, and there was nothing I could do about it. I vaguely wondered how I could keep vomiting like this, when I had hardly eaten anything that day. I could barely move, other than tilting my mouth to the side to allow the vomit to leave my body.

Then I was aware of Mam, Alison, and Denis standing in the doorway of my room. Their voices seemed to be coming from very far away. Mam came over and stood beside the bed, looking down at me.

"Jesus," Mam said. "What's wrong with her?"

"Nothing" said Alison. "She's grand. There's a bit of a bug going around and she must have picked it up. Go on out, Mam, for a minute, and I'll take care of her."

"I don't know," said Mam, worried. "She doesn't look well. Would she be expecting? She was hangin' around with that fella from the corner."

"She'll be grand," said Alison, pushing Mam out the door. "I'll sort her out."

"Okay," said Mam. "I'll go and say a prayer for her. You let me know if she gets any worse, and if she does, I'll bring her to the doctor."

Once Mam was gone, Alison and Denis started to panic. They pushed me and cajoled me and slapped my face, trying to get me to sit up. I could hear and understand what they were saying, but I just could not move. I was still sick the next morning, so they took me to hospital – I cannot remember how we got there – and told the triage nurses in A&E that I had come home in this state, and that they didn't know what was wrong with me. I am sure that the nurse had seen it all before and knew exactly what was going on, especially because Alison and Denis were themselves on the gear and off their heads.

"I think it was heroin," I managed to say to the doctor inspecting me. "Someone gave me something to take, and I think it was heroin, but I'm not sure."

Out of it as I was, I knew enough not to get Alison and Denis into trouble and I did not tell anyone that they were the ones who had given me the drug. Despite my confusion, I knew that I was the only one responsible for my predicament. I had decided to try the heroin, and if I had not done it with Alison and Denis, it would have been just a matter of time before I tried it with someone else. It was really my fault, not theirs.

I was admitted to hospital on a Tuesday and woke up on Thursday. I have absolutely no memory of anything that happened in between; I presume the hospital gave me something to counteract the effects of the heroin, to stop me from vomiting, and to rehydrate me. When I left, my hair was still in the ponytail I had been wearing when I went in. The vomit had dried out and my hair stank and was as hard and solid as a rock. The doctor who discharged me told me that I had been in a very bad way when I came in, and warned me to stay away from drugs, because clearly, I was not able to handle them and I could easily die the next time.

"You're a very lucky girl," he said, "that your auntie and uncle had the good sense to watch out for you and to take you to the hospital. If they had been less responsible, we could have been looking at a very different outcome here."

When I got home, Alison said that she was sorry she had not been taking care of me, and that I could have died. She said that she had got an awful fright and that she would kill me if I ever took heroin again.

"You'd better stay away from that stuff," Alison said contritely. "It doesn't agree with you. You don't have the constitution for it."

I don't know what Alison and Denis told Mam about what had happened, or why I was in hospital, but whatever it was, it did the job, because she never knew that I had tried heroin, or that they had given it to me.

I swore that I would never go near heroin again, and I never have, even though it was everywhere in my family and in the neighbourhood where I grew up. I am quite sure that the terrible reaction I had to the heroin that night was a sign that my parents were watching over me from heaven, and intervening so as to teach me a lesson and keep me safe.

Looking back now, I do not believe for a moment that Denis and Alison gave me the heroin on a whim or because they really thought that it would help me with my period cramps. They were both heavily addicted, and they were always desperate for money to feed their addiction. They also knew that I was going to come into a large sum of money in a few months' time. I believe that they were thinking – insofar as they were able to think at all at the time – that I would also become addicted to heroin, and that we would all be able to use my pot of money to feed our drug habit.

I do not feel angry with Alison and Denis for offering me heroin. I just feel sad. They were good people – Alison was a wonderful young woman in so many ways, and Denis had always been kind and generous to me. I know that they both loved me, as I loved them. The problem was that the heroin had taken them over, and they were no longer capable of thinking for themselves. Unless you have lived with an addict, it can be hard to understand the impact that the drug-taking has on them – but I have seen it at first hand, and I know how heroin can rot away someone's sense of self-worth and integrity from the inside, until they are prepared to do almost anything to get their next fix.

8

Money of my Own

Shortly after my one and only experiment with heroin, an opportunity to work as a receptionist at a hostel for the homeless turned up through a friend of my Auntie Edel.

"You might as well take it, love," Mam said. "Sure, you've nothing else to do, have you, and it'll be a bit of work experience for you and will help you to keep your mind off your troubles. I can manage here."

I did not think there was much point in doing the job as my money was coming soon, but I took it to keep Mam happy and to get out of the house. I reasoned that my aunties and uncles might be less critical of me if I was working, and that at least maybe then they would back off and leave me alone if I was able to show them that I was trying to do something with my life and to contribute to the household expenses.

On my first day, I met a man called John. He was a kind, fatherly man of about 50 who had been involved in building the hostel and was now working there as a janitor and care-taker. He was nice, but I didn't pay him much attention; he just seemed like any other middle-aged man at first. John was from Mayo, in the west of Ireland, and I liked his accent, which was very different to the way my Dublin family spoke.

I had only been working at the hostel for a day or two when Denis started turning up, asking me for money so that he could buy heroin. He was out of control, and started to get very insistent. John intervened to protect me. He pushed Denis out the door and told him to leave me alone, telling him that I was just a young girl trying to do my job.

I started to look at John in a different way after the incident with Denis. I liked the idea of someone who could take care of me and decided that John was the one person who could offer me a route out of the hell that I was enduring with my family at home.

John was not only kind and protective, but also handsome, even if he was from a different generation to me. I felt that John could be my dad and my boyfriend at the same time. I know that that sounds strange, but for some reason I was sure that John would protect me, and that he would be able to offer me a safe haven from the rest of my life where I would feel safe and loved . Something told me that John was someone I could rely on, and that he would never let me down. Even though I knew that I was about to come into a large sum of money, I felt trapped in my grandparents' house, and was sure that I would never be allowed to leave on my own. Suddenly, John seemed to offer me an escape route, and I trusted him not to be interested in me for the money I was about to receive. I just had to persuade John to notice me and start thinking about me in a romantic way.

John was living in a flat on Dorset Street on the north side of the inner city. Marino – where I lived with Mam and Grandad – was not that far away from his place, so he kindly started offering me a lift home after work. On the way back, in John's car, we chatted about this and that. John was softly spoken and gentle in his manner, and I started to imagine how lovely it would be to take care of a house for a man like John, to have him come home to me every evening, tired but happy to see me. By now I knew he was a father, who shared joint custody of his four children with their mother. That did not bother me at all. I thought it would be a real pleasure to cook for him, wash his clothes, and go out to the local pub with him for a few drinks at the weekend. I imagined myself putting on fresh lipstick when I knew that he was due home, so that I would look pretty for him.

Poor John had absolutely no idea what I was thinking. As the days passed, I became progressively more obsessed with him and started coming up with a plan to persuade him to be my boyfriend. When I had my own money, I thought, John would understand that I was a woman of independent means, and would respect me as a fellow adult.

On the day of my 18th birthday, I turned up at work full of excitement.

"Today's the day!" I said.

"What day is it?" John asked.

"Today's the day I get all my money!" I said. I had already told John about the compensation money that was coming to me. "You're lookin' at a wealthy woman here!"

"Be careful, Lisa," John said. "That's a lot of money for a very young girl. You'd want to get some advice on how to manage that."

"Sure, it'll be grand," I said breezily. "I can manage. I'm not a baby. I'm an adult."

I had an appointment to meet the solicitor at half past three, so I left work early and walked over to the solicitor's office in Sunlight Chambers on Parliament Street in the city centre. The solicitor was a man called Tony Hanahoe, and he had been taking care of my money all this time, after being appointed to the Stardust victims by the official government tribunal in 1982.

The Sunlight Chambers is one of the most distinctive buildings in Dublin, with art-deco tiles depicting scenes of people at work. I was quite intimidated by the grandeur of it all.

I can still remember the smell of the old building as I walked up the stairs towards the solicitors' office. It smelled of old paper, of ink, and of the dust that hung in the rays of sunlight piercing the grimy old windows. My excitement mounted as I got closer to the office. Portraits of earlier solicitors hung on the walls outside the office, looking down at me with imposing severity and full of their own importance. I felt very small and reminded myself that I was there because I was important too: I was the only orphan of the Stardust fire, here to receive compensation from the Irish government for her terrible loss.

"Come in, miss," Tony Hanahoe said, opening the door. He was a handsome and very distinguished-looking man in a three-piece suit. Grandad had told me that Mr Hanahoe was married to a Rose of Tralee and that she was a real looker. "You're very welcome."

"Call me Lisa," I said with a nervous laugh.

"Hello, Lisa," he said kindly. "Come on in and take a seat."

I went in and sat down as Mr Hanahoe went round to his own imposing chair, which creaked as he sat down. He was holding an expensive-looking gold fountain pen in his right hand.

"So today's the big day, then," he said. "At last. I bet you felt that this day would never come, eh, Lisa? The last time I saw you, you were this size."

Mr Hanahoe indicated with his hand how big I had been when he had seen me last, whether at a tribunal meeting or in the newspaper, I do not know.

"I suppose," I said.

I did not want to sit and chat with Mr Hanahoe. I just wanted him to give me my money.

Mr Hanahoe started to explain about where the money had come from, where it had been invested, and how much I was getting. All I could think about was getting the cheque so that I could leave and get on with my new life as a rich woman.

"It would be a good idea for you to talk to someone about how to invest the money," Mr Hanahoe advised. "Someone who can help you to ensure the best return on it."

"Yeah, that's okay," I said. "I don't need any help. I have a great friend. His name is John, and he's a builder."

"It's a *lot* of money, Lisa," Mr Hanahoe said. "And you're very young still. You should really talk to a professional financial advisor who can help you to get the most of it."

"There's no need, thanks," I said. "Honestly, I'm grand. I can take care of things on my own. I know what I'm doing."

Mr Hanahoe sighed deeply and shook his head. I felt very patronised. He took out the chequebook and signed the cheque over to me. Then he took out a manila envelope and put it inside.

"*Please* talk to someone you trust about the money," he said. "You could set yourself up for life if you're careful and sensible. I know this will never make up to you for losing your parents, but you can give yourself a good start in life and provide some security for yourself and any children you might have in the future."

"Thanks, Mr Hanahoe," I said, impatiently. "I really appreciate it."

"Go down to a man called Dan O'Driscoll," Mr Hanahoe said. "He works at the Allied Irish Bank on Capel Street. Go in and give that to Dan, and he can give you an advance on it to keep you going until it clears."

"That's great," I said. "Thank you very much."

I left the Sunlight Chambers with a cheque for the best part of a quarter of a million pounds in my hand, and went straight to Capel Street. I was so excited, I skipped all the way there, down the quay and across the bridge to the bank. Mr O'Driscoll was delighted to lodge my cheque for me, and he gave me an advance of £1500.

"Don't spend it all at once, love," he said with a wink. "I know what you girls are like."

"Don't you worry, Mr O'Driscoll," I said. "I'm very good at spending money. It's going to be absolutely no bother to me – I can guarantee you that!"

I grabbed my advance and dashed over to the Jervis Street Shopping Centre, where I blew a huge chunk of it on clothes, cosmetics, and perfume. It was as though the shops were calling to me; I will never forget it. I went into Oasis and grabbed one of everything that caught my eye. I went into a fancy shoe shop and exchanged my scruffy work shoes for a pair of gorgeous high heels, which I put on immediately.

I felt like a millionaire coming out of that shopping centre with my bags stuffed to the brim with pretty things. By the time I had got home, my new shoes had cut my feet to ribbons and I had destroyed them with blood; the scars from those shoes are actually visible on my feet to this day. I should have taken that as a warning but, of course, I thought nothing of it.

When I got home with my shopping bags and my big news, all of my aunts and uncles came over to give me advice on what I should do with my enormous windfall. I did not want to discuss it with anyone, and did not listen to anyone's advice, even though several of them were making very good suggestions that I would have done well to heed.

The first thing I did was to promise a substantial share to Mam and Grandad as soon as the cheque cleared, both as a way of saying thank you to them for raising me – especially to Mam, who had always loved me with all her heart – and as a way of showing the whole family that I no longer had to feel beholden to anybody. I also promised a monetary gift to each of my aunts and uncles – even those with a heroin problem, although I was concerned that they would use it to buy drugs and kill themselves.

"Don't go mad with the money, Lisa, love," Mam said. "Don't spend it all at once. I know it's a lot of money, but if you go mad, you'll find it disappears awful quick. If you're sensible, the money could make such a big difference to your life."

"I won't," I promised. "I'll be sensible."

We both knew that that was never going to happen. I had always been much better at spending money than saving it and I was 18 – how many 18 year olds are good at planning for the future?

Shortly after I turned 18 and cashed my big cheque, John took me out for a drink to Kenny's pub, which was near the hostel where we both worked.

"What would you like, pet?" John asked as we went in.

"I'd like a Bacardi, please," I said.

John got me a Bacardi and a Black Bush whiskey for himself, and we both sat down at a little table in the corner.

"The thing is, John," I said, "I really like you."

"You're a great girl," John said, in an avuncular manner. He patted the back of my hand. "I bet your family is really proud of you."

"No, John," I said. "I mean I *really* like you. I mean, I *like* like you."

John just stared at me over his glass, his blue eyes widening in alarm.

"What are you talking about?" he asked.

"I want you to be my boyfriend, John. We'll be boyfriend and girlfriend. Won't that be nice?"

John stared at me for ages, and then he put his whiskey down very carefully on the coaster in front of him and took a deep breath.

"Oh, Jesus no, love," John said. "Oh God, no. That wouldn't do at all. I'll always be there for you, but no... just no. It wouldn't be right. You're way too young for me. You're little more than a child."

"I mean it!" I said defiantly. "I think I'd be a brilliant girlfriend for you. I'd make you very happy. Give me a chance and I'll show you."

"Love, you're only just after having one sup of your drink," John said. "What's wrong with you?"

"I'm not drunk!" I said indignantly. "I know exactly what I am saying, and I know exactly what I want, and what I want is you."

John was so shocked, we just finished our drinks and then he took me home, hardly saying a word to me all the way back.

Despite John's shock, I was not taking no for an answer. Over the next few weeks, I kept insisting that I wanted John, and that eventually I was going to have him, whether he accepted it or not. I would sneak up on him and put my arms around him to give him a hug. Eventually he started hugging me back. I am so glad he was there for me then because I was coming under so much pressure from all sides now that I had the money. Even John could not stop me from making mistakes, but he did advise me to be careful, and made sure that he was there to help me fight my corner.

John and I had met in the summer, and all autumn long I continued my campaign to become his girlfriend. That Christmas, he went back to Mayo to visit his family. I tried ringing him over and over again that Christmas, but he never answered his phone. When he eventually returned to Dublin, I was very indignant, even though John had not agreed to my plan that we should be in a relationship with one another. He had, in fact, made it quite clear that he felt we should not get involved.

"Where were you?" I shouted down the phone when John came back from visiting his family and I was eventually able to speak with him. "I've been waiting for you for weeks! I didn't know where you were. Did you not realise that I would be worried about you?"

"Calm down, Lisa," John said. "I was just visiting my mother for Christmas. Look, do you want to meet for a meal or something and we can talk things over?"

John and I arranged to meet at a restaurant in Portobello, a trendy area on the south side of the city. As soon as we sat down, I put my arms around him and refused to let him go.

"Ah, Jesus, Lisa," John said. "I can't be your boyfriend, you know that. I've been thinking about it over Christmas, and I know it's not right. I'm an old man, compared to you! What would people think?"

"I don't care what they think!" I said. "I love you and that's all that matters. I think you love me too – and even if you don't love me yet, I know that you can learn to."

"What's wrong with you?" John said. "There's loads of young lads out there dying to have a pretty girlfriend like you. You shouldn't be wasting your time with an auld fella like me. It doesn't make any sense."

"But I don't *want* them," I said, pouting. "I only want *you*. You are exactly the boyfriend that I have always dreamed of. I think that you are absolutely perfect."

"Oh, merciful Jesus Christ," John said. "I can't. It wouldn't be good. People would talk about us. They'd think I'm a dirty old man or something."

"No, John," I said. "I want you and that's all there is to it. I'm going to have you, and I'm not giving you any choice."

All evening, I made my case to John. I pointed out that I had been out of school for over two years now, that I had my own money, that I was over 18 when the age of consent in Ireland was 17, and that I could do whatever I wanted.

"Okay," John said eventually. "We'll take it slow and see how it goes."

I squealed with joy and hugged John again, almost overcome with excitement. I knew with every fibre of my being that this was the right thing for me.

After the meal, John and I went to a nearby pub, Conn's of Camden Street, for a drink. Conn, who owned the place, was a real old-school publican who knew John and enjoyed a bit of banter with him.

"Now, who's this lovely lady?" Conn asked, as he wiped down the counter where we were standing.

"This is my friend," John said bashfully. "Her name is Lisa."

"No," I said firmly. "I'm his girlfriend. Very nice to meet you."

I extended my hand to shake Conn's. He took my hand and inspected my face. Conn's eyebrows raised so high they nearly disappeared behind his hair.

"What?" he said. "Jesus, John, she's awful young. Are you sure about this?"

"Yeah, but he's my boyfriend anyway," I said. "And I'm actually a grown woman, thank you very much. I'm not a child."

I thought that if I told everyone that John was my boyfriend, I would make it come true. John had not even kissed me yet, but I was sure that if I was determined enough, he would eventually give in to my demands and I would get all the love in the world from him. I was sure that he would never hurt me.

After our drink, John dropped me back home, as he always did. I had never seen inside his flat, because he did not feel that it would be right for him to be alone with such a young girl. But something had changed in him since I told Conn earlier that he was my boyfriend. That evening, when he stopped the car outside my house, he leaned forward and pecked me on the lips in an experimental fashion. My arms flew up, and I grabbed him either side of the face and pressed his mouth against mine. I nearly swallowed him up. I wanted so badly for John to kiss me that I would have done anything I could to make him come closer to me.

"Jesus, Lisa," John said, when he eventually got away. "Take it easy."

I kept up my campaign. Honestly, I do not know how he put up with me. I was like a force of nature. Eventually, I wore him down and I saw the inside of that flat. It was a real bachelor pad: small and clean but very evidently lacking a woman's touch. John's clothes were draped all over the furniture in the bedroom, and the kitchenette was filled with tea-stained cups and egg-stained plates.

"Don't mind the state of the place," said John. "It's not much of a home. I'm almost always at work, so it's really just a place to sleep."

John took me down to Mayo, where he still worked sometimes, and where his mother still lived. We were going to stay in a hotel – he did not feel ready to introduce me to his family yet – and I still remember how embarrassed John was about booking a room for us, as though someone might jump out of the wardrobe and accuse him of kidnapping me from my parents. He suggested getting a room with twin beds. I told him he had to be joking, that I was his girlfriend now, and consequently I expected to sleep in a big bed, with him. I got so upset, I burst into tears, because I thought that if John did not want to be with me the way I wanted, that meant that I was not good enough for someone like him to love. Once again, after a lot of wheedling on my part, John gave in – and the rest is history.

Shortly after our first trip away, I asked John if I could tell my family about our relationship and start bringing it out into the open. He was very nervous, understandably, but he agreed. I was hopeful that Mam would be accepting because she knew John a little bit from him dropping me home after work, and she had formed a favourable opinion of him.

"That's a lovely man," Mam had often said of John. "It's real kind of him to leave you home after work. He's a decent sort."

"Yeah, he is lovely," I had always said. "He'd give you the shirt off his back."

Now that John had given me permission to tell people about our relationship, the next time Mam said that John was a lovely man, I had my opening.

"Yeah, he is lovely," I said. "And he's my boyfriend now. We've been together for a few weeks. I was just waiting for the right moment to tell you."

Mam laughed a little uncertainly. Then she looked at me again and realised that I was actually serious.

"Get fuckin' over," she said. "Sure, he's a bleedin' old man. What are you talking about, Lisa? Are you after havin' one drink too many?"

"He is my boyfriend," I said stoutly. "And I love him."

"What are you talkin' about?" said Mam. "You couldn't spell love! You wouldn't know love if it came up and slapped you in the face! Will you stop? It's nonsense you're talking."

"I'm not going to continue this conversation if you're not going to believe me," I said, full of indignation.

I was hurt because I had really hoped that Mam would feel happy for me and would be delighted to know that John was in my life now and that I was no longer alone. I left the room and walked out into the hall, ready to go outside where John was waiting on the corner, in the car.

Mam wheezed, got out of her chair and followed me, tapping me on the shoulder emphatically.

"Come on, now, Lisa," she said. "This isn't right. You have my heart scalded, love. You're only a young girl and he's more than old enough to be your father. If you can't see sense, I'll bring you to the best psychiatrist in Dublin and we'll get you sorted. It isn't normal for a young girl to want to go out with a man of that age."

"I don't need any psychiatrist," I said. "I have John! John will take care of me. He understands me. The time for me to see a psychiatrist was years ago, when he might have taken me out of this kip of a house."

"I can't believe what you're saying," Mam said. "You're not well. There's something wrong with you. It's not right. What will people say?"

"No, I *am* well," I insisted. "I am totally well, and I've never been better than I am now. I've finally found someone who really understands me, and I know he'll always be there for me."

I went upstairs and stuffed an armful of my pretty new clothes into a bag, along with a few fistfuls of make-up and perfume. Then I stomped downstairs and, shouting over my shoulder that I would be staying with John if anyone needed me, I left. As soon as John and I got back to his flat, I started reorganising John's things to make the place look nicer and to show him that I meant business.

I gave up my job at the hostel, convinced that I had enough compensation money to set me up for life, and spent the next few months enjoying the new car I had bought – a brand-new Honda Civic – buying clothes, and enjoying the blissful feeling of being in love for the first time.

I was still friendly with the same kids I had been pals with in school, especially Maria and Nikki McConnell. I told Maria and Nikki all about John and they said they were dying to meet him. I eventually arranged for us all to go out for dinner together.

"Be on your best behaviour," I warned my friends. "You're meeting John for the first time and I want him to like you. Don't make faces at me in front of John, or make faces at him. I'll go ballistic if you do!"

"Can't wait to see this John fella," Maria said. "We've been very curious about him."

Maria, Nikki, and I were already sitting in the restaurant when John came in. He had dressed smartly for the occasion in jeans, well-cut shoes, and a tweed blazer.

I nudged Maria.

"There's John now," I said. "That's him, just after coming in."

Maria burst out laughing.

"Stop kiddin' me," she said. "That can't be him. That's not a boyfriend; that's someone's da! You're a mad yoke, Lisa! You're pullin' our leg. You nearly had me goin' there for a minute."

"No, it is," I insisted. "That's my John, and I love him."

I could feel my face turning red with anger as I felt disrespected by my friends; I wanted so much for them to approve of my choice and to like John. Maria stopped laughing and looked me, her eyebrows raised quizzically.

"Are you fuckin' serious?" she asked. "That's really John? Like, for real? You're actually goin' out with him?"

"I've never been more serious in my bleedin' life," I told her, annoyed.

"If you're happy, I'm happy," Maria said.

"Me too," said Nikki.

The three of us shared a hug as John walked over.

That was just the first of many occasions when people cast doubt on my conviction that John was the man for me.

John said hello and sat down beside me and opposite Maria and Nikki. I could see that he was nervous and even intimidated by my teenage friends. After a few minutes, though, everyone relaxed and we were able to talk, and before long Maria and Nikki could see that John really was a good person who loved me and had my best interests at heart.

Unfortunately, my family struggled to accept my relationship with John for quite some time. They accused him of being after my money, said that he was just a phase that I was going through, and that I should buck up and see sense. Grandad agreed with this point of view:

"You get the fuck away from him," Grandad said. "He's three times your age. It's not normal. It's not right. What are you like, going around with him?"

"I don't care what I'm like," I said, defiantly. "I'm stayin' with John and I'm getting out of this kip and away from you. We love each other, and that's all there is to it. If you don't like it, you can fuck off."

All I could do was tell my family that I loved John, trusted him, and that everything would be all right. I knew that John would never leave me – and I knew that there was a lot of resentment towards me now that I finally had my money and could afford to buy a new car and all the clothes I wanted.

Now that I had John, while I still suffered from anxiety at least I felt secure in the knowledge that someone cared about me and was prepared to be there for me, no matter what. This gave me a little headspace, and I was able to acknowledge that I needed help with my anxiety and other psychological problems. Mam had been advising me to see someone for years, but I had not wanted to hear about it. Now I accepted that she was right, and I could also afford to pay the fees, so I arranged to attend a psychologist in the hope that I would learn how to understand myself better, and how to come to terms with my parents' deaths and all the other things that had happened in the family over the years.

The psychologist was a softly-spoken, kind woman with a dark grey bob and sharp eyes behind her glasses. I can still remember the smell of the incense she burned in her office. Talking did help, a little. My anxiety receded, but it never completely went away. I hoped that, with John's support, I would gradually learn how to feel confident about myself and my place in the world.

I know that John and I have sometimes been judged harshly because of the big age difference between us. It was always very frustrating for me when people – especially people I cared about – queried my relationship with him or suggested that it was not real and meaningful because he was so much older than me. I would like to make it clear that John has never once taken advantage of me; not then, and never since. To this day, I am grateful that I met John, because he is the only person in my life who has really tried to understand me, and how I have always lived in the shadow of the Stardust flames. He is the only person who has never let me down. No matter what happens between us, I will always love him.

9

Life with John

Now that I am older, I have more understanding of my grand-parents' concerns when I started going out with John. Then, I was impatient with them for not immediately embracing the relationship and accepting John into the family. Now, I can see that many of the things they said were true: I was very young to want to settle down; John was really far too old for me, and I had very little life experience on which to base such a big decision, especially after having dropped out of school and severely limiting my future prospects by refusing to take my education seriously.

I can also understand that my grandparents were concerned that the money might make me vulnerable, although I knew this was never a factor as far as John was concerned. But I was also utterly sure – even if I could not explain where the certainty came from – that John would always be there for me, no matter what, and I could only hope that eventually Mam and Grandad would come around and accept him into the fold.

At the time, John advised me to be patient and to give my grandparents time to get used to the idea that he and I were together as a couple. He was older and wiser than me, and he understood where they were coming from. He also did not fully understand how abusive my grandfather could be, although I had tried to tell him.

"They're just watching out for you, love," John said philosophically. "Sure, I'd be the same if one of my own girls wanted to go out with an older man. I'd be raging. Give them some time and I'm sure they'll come around."

After John and I had been together for a few months, I thought it was time to give Mam and Grandad a chance to get to know him, so I suggested that they let us take them out for the day. I wanted Mam in particular to see John for the wonderful person he was, and to understand why I loved him so much. I wanted her to smile at us both and to reassure me that she was happy with the choices I had made.

Despite my grandfather's behaviour towards me at times, I wanted his approval as well. I knew that my decision to go out with John was controversial in the family, and felt that if Grandad gave us his blessing, it would probably make things easier for me with everyone else.

With some misgivings, Mam and Grandad agreed to meet John. We arranged to go to Skerries, a pretty seaside town in north County Dublin that is always very popular with day-trippers from the city. John and I took them out for lunch and drinks in a popular pub.

As soon as we all sat down for lunch, John started the conversation by apologising for getting involved with me, even though I had told him that there was no need for him to feel embarrassed or ashamed; I had been the one doing all the running, and our relationship had been my idea in the first place.

"Jesus," John said. "I'm very sorry about this. I didn't want to be with this girl at the start, you know. I did my best to get away from her. I want you to know that. None of this was my idea in the first place. It all came from her."

"What do you mean?" Mam asked. "How did you try to get away from her?"

"I'm so old compared to her," John said. "I know it doesn't look right. I told her so a million times, but she just wouldn't stop asking me... she's very insecure... and eventually, I got fond of the girl. It's very hard to say no to her."

"God help my Lisa," Mam said. "She's always suffered something terrible with her anxiety. She lives on her nerves, that girl. I just hope that you'll be able to help her with it. She needs an awful lot of support. Things don't come easy to her."

"I'll do my best," John assured her. "I really do love her, you know. I know it's been very hard on her, losing her mother and father and all that. I think she feels that she needs a strong man whose shoulder she can lean on. For whatever reason, she seems to feel that I'm the one she wants."

"Well, if there's one thing I know about my Lisa," said Mam, "it's that when her heart is set on something, she'll do anything to make sure she gets it. So I suppose that if you're what she wants, then you had little chance of getting away from her."

Mam and John clinked their glasses together in agreement, and I smiled. I could see that Mam was getting used to the idea of John being around. I had been sure that he would win her over just by being himself, and I was right.

By the time lunch was over, Mam and Grandad could see for themselves that John really was a kind and generous person and that he had nothing but my best interests at heart. They were still not thrilled about me going out with him, because of the huge age difference, but they had decided to accept it and to trust that I was making the right decision. In any case, they could see that I had made my mind up, and that nothing they could do or say was going to change it.

Before long, Mam had actually become very fond of John, and a month or two after our outing to Skerries, she told me that, no matter what some people might say about us, our relationship had her blessing.

"When it comes to love," Mam said, "age is just a number. If the love is there, it's no more important than the number on your door. I wasn't sure about this John fella at first, but now I can see that he makes you happy, and I'm glad you found one another. I hope that your life will seem less of a burden to you now that he is in it."

It was also time for me to meet John's mother, Mary Jane. His father had passed away some time before, but his mother still lived in the homeplace in rural County Mayo and John went down to visit her quite often.

I was on tenterhooks the whole way to Mayo, as John left Dublin and drove west.

"Oh God, John," I fretted. "What if she doesn't like me? I know you love your mother; will you leave me if she doesn't like me?"

"Of course she'll like you," he reassured me. "What is there not to like? She's going to love you. I like you, don't I?"

"I don't know, John," I said. "I've a feeling she won't want me in the house, and we'll have to turn around and go back the way we came. She'll say I'm too young for you or something. Or maybe that she doesn't like girls from Dublin and thinks you should be with a Mayo woman. I'll be mortified. I'll want the ground to open up and swallow me."

"Not a bit of it," said John. "Wasn't my own father 20 years older than her, and they had a great marriage. I am sure she won't have a problem with it. The way I see it is, if we're half as happy in our relationship as they were in theirs, we'll be doing grand."

Eventually, after hours of driving on the narrow country roads – they seemed so strange to me, the city girl, with the thick growth of trees and bushes overhanging them, and punctuated only occasionally by an isolated farmhouse – we arrived.

"Home sweet home," said John as he drove up to the front door and parked. He put on the handbrake and turned the key in the ignition to turn off the engine. For a moment, we both just sat there, looking out the windscreen.

I looked curiously at my surroundings. It was all very strange to me. We were such city people in my family that we rarely ever ventured to the countryside, and I knew nothing about how country people lived. Phoenix Park in Dublin was the countryside, so far as we were concerned. I wondered what it must have been like to grow up in a place where there were more sheep than people. It was hard for me to imagine getting up every morning and opening the curtains only to see green fields, trees, and animals rather than bricks and mortar.

John's family home was a cute little cottage in the countryside, surrounded by farmland. His dad had worked a small farm before he died, providing his family with a modest but steady income. The land was rented out now, but Mary Jane had decided to stay on because the little house had been her home ever since she was a young bride and she had so many happy memories of raising her family there. She was standing near the window when we pulled up, and her sweet, old face broke into a smile as soon as she saw us.

I panicked the moment I saw Mary Jane, and realised that she was waving at us to come in.

"Oh Jesus, John," I said. "I'm scared she won't like me. I'm just going to stay in the car. You go in without me. I'll be grand here. I'll just sit here and wait for you. I don't want to be any bother."

"Are you joking?" he said, exasperated. "I'm after driving three and a half hours to get you here. The least you can do is get out and say hello to my mother. Sure, she's been only dying to meet you. You're not going to disappoint her, are you?"

Awkwardly, I got out of the car and gave Mary Jane a shy smile.

"Hello, *a stór*," she said. "You're very welcome here."

A stór is an Irish term of affection that Mayo people use all the time. It can be translated as "my darling" or "my dear".

"Hello," I said nervously, in a very small voice. "It's nice to meet you."

"Loosen up, will you?" John said. "This is my mother, not the Spanish Inquisition!"

Mary Jane led us into the house, full of smiles. I think that John must have told her how nervous I was, because she went out of her way to be kind and welcoming. The little house was warm and cosy, and smelled of turf smoke, freshly baked bread, and strawberry jam.

"Sit down, my love," Mary Jane said. She patted the sofa and smiled at me invitingly. Nervously, I sat down in the spot she indicated.

John was fed up with me being timid, and he got right to the point.

"Mammy," he said, "where's Lisa going to sleep tonight? Will she sleep on the couch? Or maybe I should make up a bed for her in the shed outside?"

"John!" I said, horrified. "Don't you dare! Not in front of your mother!"

I went bright red and stared fixedly at my shoes, wishing that the floor would open up and swallow me – anything to get away from my embarrassment. I could not believe that

John was discussing the matter of us going to bed together with his mother.

"Oh, Jesus, no," Mary Jane said. "Would you give it over? She's with you now, so she's sleeping with you. Sure, you're a couple now, aren't you?"

John and his mother chatted, and I gradually relaxed as I looked around the living room. In some ways, it was a little like my grandmother's house: there was a picture of the Sacred Heart on the wall, and the mantelpiece and occasional table held a substantial collection of holy statues and bottles of holy water. While she was clearly very broad-minded, Mary Jane was also a very traditional woman in many ways, and her faith was extremely important to her. I found this reassuring because it reminded me of Mam, and how her holy statues and her prayers brought her happiness too. There was comfort for me in the familiar paraphernalia of a simple and genuinely held faith.

When John went out to the kitchen to get something, his mother winked at me.

"Will you get two glasses, *a stór*," she said. "And we'll have a dropeen. Sure, a little drop never did anyone any harm, isn't that right?"

I took two glasses off the shelf that she indicated and gave them to Mary Jane, who removed a bottle of Jameson whiskey from her sideboard and poured us both a generous measure.

"Drink up, love," she said. "It'll do you good."

I had never drunk neat whiskey in my life, and I was afraid that it was going to make me cough and splutter.

"Can I have a sup of lemonade in it?" I asked. "Like, just to take the edge off?"

"No," Mary Jane said. "Certainly not. You're in Mayo now, and we don't do that down here. Lemonade indeed!"

Mary Jane chuckled, clearly highly amused by my suggestion.

I did not say another word but just sipped my whiskey and tried not to wince at the burning sensation as it went down my throat.

The next day, I met John's sister Mary and his brother-in-law, who lived about a hundred metres down the road. Once again, I was almost too scared to get out of the car, but Mary gave me a big hug and told me that I was very welcome and that if John was happy, they were happy. I also met John's other sister, Anne, who lived a drive away. Anne was warm, welcoming, and clearly very house-proud, with a beautiful home that – I would learn – always smelled of baking. I also met John's brother Jimmy and his wife Margaret, who lived in England, but were over for a visit, as well as his brother Frank and his lovely family. By the time we left Mayo, I was a little more relaxed; John's family could not have been kinder.

John had four children, and of course, as our relationship grew more serious, he wanted me to meet them so that we could get to know one another. The kids lived with their mother, from whom he had been separated for a number of years – but they also spent a lot of time with John, and I already knew how much they meant to him.

"Don't be nervous, love," John said. "They're going to love you. I have absolutely no doubt about it."

But I *was* nervous – extremely nervous. The oldest of John's children, Jane, was just a few years younger than me, and I was scared that they all would dislike me, and disapprove of my relationship with John.

John initially arranged for me to meet the eldest two kids in a pub, a casual setting that would not be intimidating for any of us.

"This is my friend Lisa," John told the children, Jane and James.

I smiled and said hello, but my heart was in my mouth. John's son was nearly as tall as me and Jane, the eldest, was 12 and already beginning to look like a teenager. The two kids eyed me speculatively.

"Is that your girlfriend, Dad?" Jane asked.

I could see from the sparkle in Jane's eye that she was a messer who would not let her dad get away with anything – and that if I gave her a chance, she would run rings around me, too.

"Not at all!" John said, flustered and feeling that he was being put on the spot. "Stop that!"

About a week later, John and I took his two younger children, Jonathan and April, out to visit my parents' graves at the cemetery in Sutton. I suppose I felt that as John was going to be in my family now, it was only right that he should know about my parents, what had happened to them, and where they were now. I think that I also felt that as my grandparents had not been very accepting of John at first, I wanted to feel a sense of approval from my parents, who I still believed were watching me from heaven and doing their best to guide me on my winding path through life. I thought that perhaps they had sent John to me, to be my guardian angel on this earth.

We parked the car alongside the railings and John and I got out and walked to the grave, with the children waiting in the car. As we approached the grave, John put his arm around me, leaned over, and kissed me on the cheek. I could feel the children's eyes watching us.

"Jesus, Lisa," said John, reading the inscriptions on my parents' gravestones. "It's an awful shame. So young." He wiped away a tear. "I'm sure they loved you, Lisa," he said. "It's just such a pity they didn't live to see you grow up."

Even though I had told John the story of my parents' deaths a hundred times, I could see how moved he was by seeing their graves. I felt a burst of emotion and love for John, who had never met Francis and Maureen, but who was now mourning them, all these years later. I had a sense of complete conviction that my parents were looking down on us, and that they approved and were happy for me.

That evening, the children asked John if I was his girlfriend, and he told them that yes, I was. I think that we had both been afraid that they would reject me, but they were open from the start. I will always be grateful to John's children for having accepted me into their family at a time when I was still very young and vulnerable.

John was a wonderful father, and it was lovely to see how patient and kind he was with his children. I envied them for the relationship they had with their father, and imagined how I might have had a similar relationship with Francis, if he had survived.

Of course, my relationship with the children did have its ups and downs. John's eldest daughter Jane was 12 years old, just six years younger than me; we could easily have been sisters. Sometimes we got a bit jealous of each other and competed for John's attention, which must have been infuriating for him. The kids had to get used to me being a regular presence in their lives, and I am sure that I made mistakes along the way – after all, I was still getting used to being a grown woman, and knew little about being a mother. However, we all made allowances for one another, and we learned how to get along.

I did my best to be a mother figure to the children when they were staying with John and me, which was not always easy. A case in point was the first time I went to a parent-teacher meeting, because John was not free. When it was my turn, I went up to Jane's teacher, and sat down in front of her.

"Excuse me, who are you?" asked the teacher, confused.

"I'm Jane's stepmother," I said.

I had put on the most grown-up clothes I had, but clearly, I was not fooling anyone.

"You can't be!" she said. "Who are you really? A sister or something? Is this some sort of a joke?"

"No, I *am* her stepmother," I insisted. "I'm here for the parent-teacher meeting because John can't make it. He asked me to come because he takes Jane's education very seriously and he wanted to be sure he heard all about her."

"You mean you're John's partner? A girlfriend of some sort?"

"Yeah, that's right. I'm John's partner. His life partner."

I tried to sound grown-up and confident, but my voice wobbled a bit. I was afraid that if she questioned me any further, I might start to cry.

The teacher looked at me uncertainly, but she went on with the meeting. She could not stop staring at me, and seemed to be in shock. I was embarrassed, but I managed to get through it.

There were many awkward moments when John and I went out together, too. One night we were enjoying a quiet drink together in a pub when a man we did not know tapped John on the shoulder.

"You go home to your bleedin' wife," the man said, "and stop hangin' around with young girls. You ought to be ashamed of yourself. Is she even legal, for God's sake? It's disgusting."

John is an even-tempered man, but he got very angry that night. I was very grateful that he was there to stand up for me because I always took criticisms like this – of either him or me – very hard.

More often, rather than people confronting us directly, we just had to hear the comments made about us as soon as we turned our backs:

"Your man must have a few bob or she wouldn't be interested in him. Gold-diggers; they're all the same, wha'?"

"Here comes the sugar-daddy. I can hear his pockets jingling from here!"

"Who does he think he is? Fuckin' Rod Stewart?"

"The little slut. Easy to see what turns *her* on."

On other occasions, people would innocently assume that I was Jane, John's oldest daughter, and would be left red-faced and embarrassed when we had to set them straight.

I didn't care about any of this and was always proud to be seen with John. I felt that John had saved me, that he was my lover and protector, and that there was nothing wrong with what we were doing. It was harder on John, who did care what people thought about him, and hated it when someone suggested that he was doing something wrong.

In retrospect, I can see that having me in John's life was much harder on his children than I realised at the time. They were sometimes embarrassed to be seen out and about with their father and his much younger girlfriend, and they were painfully aware of the fact that not everyone approved of the age difference. No doubt they were occasionally teased about it at school. Although we mostly got along well, I am sure there were some times when they would have preferred that I was not there.

It was easier playing the role of wife and stepmother at home, and in fact I enjoyed it. I tried to channel my mother, who I knew to have been very house-proud, and I did my best to keep the house looking nice (although, if I am being honest, I am not nearly as tidy and organised as I have been told Maureen was). I cooked the evening meal for John and welcomed him home every day after work. I loved doing this, and taking care of all the domestic work about the house, because this was one area in which I felt competent and in control. Mam had trained me well in the domestic arts and I knew what to do and how to turn ordinary ingredients into a tasty meal. When John finished his plate with satisfaction and thanked me for my work in the kitchen, I felt a real glow of pride.

John was very appreciative of all that I did, and nothing made me happier than seeing him smile and say thank you for a meal, or for his freshly ironed shirts. I liked the feeling that I was creating a home for his children, and did my best to provide them with a cosy and welcoming environment. Looking back now, I can see that I must have looked like a little girl playing with a dolls' house. However, I can also see that – little by little – I was growing in confidence. While I remained very anxious, being away from my family suited me, and I was beginning to grow up.

By now, not only had my grandparents accepted my relationship with John, but most of my aunts and uncles had too. This was less to do with me, and more to do with the fact that John was unfailingly generous – "giveish", as Mam described him, with one of her characteristic turns of phrase. If we were all out in a pub, he insisted on buying round after round of drinks, and if someone needed a loan or a hand-out, John was generally happy to provide. I was proud and happy to be with a man who everyone liked, and who could afford to splash out because he had a good job and worked hard. I was very proud of John's ability to provide for me and for his family.

Life with John

Mam had grown very fond of Jane, John's eldest, and sometimes she and I would stay over and sleep in my old bedroom. Jane loved Emma, too, and enjoyed playing with her and helping Alison. I was delighted by the fact that Jane was growing close to my beloved Mam, and made sure that she was kept well away from Grandad, who I still did not trust.

One night, the whole family was at a party in a function room, everyone seated around a big table. Grandad, as usual, had finished a few pints. All of a sudden, and for no reason that I could discern, Grandad started berating me in front of all of my relatives. He got angrier and angrier with me.

"You're like that tramp of a mother of yours!" Grandad finally shouted at me. "You're just out for whatever you can get. That's what she was like, and what did she finally get? She got what was coming to her. The only pity is that she took a good man down with her when she went."

I actually recoiled physically, as though Grandad had stuck a knife between my ribs. John put his arm around me, dumbstruck with horror. Up until now, he had never seen Grandad behave like this, and only knew him as a polite and entertaining older man.

"Don't you speak to Lisa like that," said one of my aunts, leaping to my defence. "That's disgraceful talk. If you've nothing nice to say, Dad, keep your mouth shut. There's no need for that. Did you never hear of 'don't speak ill of the dead'?"

Everyone else carefully avoided making eye contact with Grandad, and suddenly seemed very interested in their drinks. That is when I started to realise that not just Grandad, but many other members of the family still held a negative view of my mother, and maybe even blamed her for Francis's death. After all, he had made it out of the Stardust alive, and had run back into the flames for her. If he had not done that, he would have been alive still. Could it be, I wondered, that they were still angry with her over Francis's death? Was that why they often seemed to be so annoyed with me?

A few weeks later, during another family outing, my Aunt Mary reminisced about how she had fallen out with Francis and Maureen just a few weeks before they died. Apparently, the last thing Maureen had said to her was, "You're never seeing my Lisa again."

"Little did she know," said Mary, "that three weeks later I'd be helping to rear you."

I took great offence at what Mary said, and lunged at her, with the intention of slapping her or doing something to shock her. Fortunately, John held me back and talked some sense into me. Mary apologised later that evening for having upset me, but her words still hung in the air between us, poisoning everything.

When someone dies, everyone's relationship with them remains in a state of stasis. If Maureen and Francis had not been killed in the Stardust disaster, whatever silly disagreement they had had with Mary would probably have been forgotten within weeks. Life would have moved on. But because their lives were cut short, and the argument remained unresolved, Mary had been left with regrets that had never gone away.

Life with John

* * *

I had told a few people about the strange way Grandad behaved at times, but I always had the impression that nobody quite believed me, or thought that I was just being mean to him. I couldn't really blame them, because his behaviour could be so strange that I could hardly believe it myself. Even John, who always supported me, was doubtful and wondered if I had misheard him, or was exaggerating. It was very difficult for anyone to comprehend that my grandfather — who was to most people a well-spoken, sociable man who would talk to anyone down the pub and who was never contrary with anyone other than his own family members — could behave in such a way in his own home.

Then, one night, John and I were staying at Mam and Grandad's, and after we had gone to bed, Grandad started walking up the stairs loudly saying, "Alison and Lisa, I'll show youse what it's all about tonight. That'll sort the two of youse out."

Then Grandad came into my room and stood over the bed.

"Pretend I'm John," he said to me.

I realised that, as it was dark, Grandad did not realise that John was there beside me.

John jumped out of the bed. I'll never forget the look of utter shock and horror on his face. Grandad just turned around and walked out, as mortified and embarrassed as I was.

"Lisa," John said. "Let's get out of here. I don't think your grandfather is quite right in the head."

Although I was absolutely mortified, part of me was glad that John had heard what Grandad said, because now I knew I wasn't going mad.

*   *   *

Despite everything, Grandad was still the only father figure I had ever had, and even though his behaviour towards me had become very upsetting in recent years, I could see that he really did love Mam, and always had. I still hoped that I could make things right between us, so one evening I invited him out for a drink – just the two of us. Grandad said he wanted a pint of Guinness, so I got his drink and put it down in front of him. Before either of us took a sip, I laid my cards out on the table and spoke to him plainly.

"Listen," I said, "I know you're getting old and you're pissed off with the way things have turned out for the family, and life is hard, but I don't like the way you talk to me, and it's been going on for a long time now. I'm scared of you. Those things you say – they're not right. I haven't had a full night's sleep in this house for years."

"Sorry," Grandad said. "I'm just fed up in that house. I'll try to do better. I'm only messin' with you."

"It doesn't feel like messin' to me," I said. "I know you like to have a few drinks and you've had problems in your life, but you've got to stop scaring me."

Grandad hunched his shoulders and stared down miserably at his pint. I could see that he felt extremely uncomfortable, and had the impression that he really was sorry about his behaviour.

"The problems in the house are not my fault," I said. "And you shouldn't be saying those things to me. It's not much to ask."

"Just don't say anything to any of the others," he said. "And I won't do it again. I promise."

Grandad's strange behaviour eased off somewhat after that, but I never really trusted him again.

* * *

John kept begging me to be more careful with all the compensation money I had received. Although I took his advice with some of it, and invested in a property development scheme, I spent the rest as though it was never going to end. It is amazing how quickly you can spend money if you put your mind to it. I exchanged my Honda Civic for a Rover Executive ("Merciful Jesus Christ," said Mam, when I pulled up outside the house, "she thinks she's a celebrity"), and I bought myself beautiful new clothes every week. Just two years after Mr Hanahoe had handed me my enormous cheque, I had no ready access to money, although the property investment would provide John and me with income a few years later. I was still very immature and naïve, and did not see a problem, or understand how stupid I had been with much of the money; I knew that John was a hard worker, and trusted him to support me now that my nest-egg had been largely frittered away. I had no doubt that he would always be there for me.

I am embarrassed and ashamed now to look back and admit how careless I was with so much of the money that I was given. I could have bought a house or set up a little business for myself. There are hundreds of better uses I could have made of it. I know that I have to take responsibility for my mistakes. The only thing I can say in my own defence is that I was very young, and I do not think most 18 year olds have the maturity to make wise decisions about their financial future.

The Stardust Campaign held an event for the 20th anniversary of the fire. There was a ceremony at which a bouquet of flowers was given to the family members of those who died: one bouquet for each of the 48 victims. I was given two great big bunches of flowers: one for each of my parents. I clutched them in my arms and cried as I walked through the crowd to John, who was waiting to comfort me.

Now that I was grown up, I wanted to find out more about the campaign for justice for the victims of the Stardust fire and their families. All this time, the campaign had been working hard, trying to get the fire investigated properly, and trying – even after all these years – to make sure that whoever was responsible for the tragedy faced justice.

The Irish public all knew the names of the lead campaigners, who frequently went to the media with calls for a new inquest into the disaster. They were sure that the 1982 inquest had been, at worst, a cover-up and, at best, an example of incompetence.

When I was a child, Mam had deliberately kept me away from the campaign most of the time, because I received a lot of media attention as it was, and she wanted to protect me and let me have as normal a childhood as she could provide. Now, I arranged to meet, for the first time as an adult, Antoinette Keegan, who together with her mother, Chrissie, was one of the main organisers of the campaign. Antoinette was a survivor of the fire that had killed her two beautiful teenage sisters, and an absolutely tireless advocate for all the families that had been affected; her mother had lived with the pain of losing two children ever since.

Antoinette and Chrissie could not have been kinder to me. I can still remember Chrissie's warm arms around me as she gave me a hug and told me that she was absolutely sure that my parents were looking down on me and that they loved me. I told them that I wanted to help, and that I would fight alongside them. They were delighted, because I had been given so much attention by the media as the only orphan of the tragedy, and I was in a good position to become the posterchild of the campaign. I was also young and pretty, and they had spent enough time around the media to know that that never hurt when it came to deciding which photos would make the front page of the newspaper, and which footage would be considered interesting enough for the evening news.

My aunts and uncles accused me of wanting to be involved as a way of drawing more attention to myself, saying that I was being a show-off and that I thought I was great. I could not understand this: who needed a reason to get involved in a campaign for justice for their dead parents? Nonetheless, I went to a few meetings, all fired up with the idea that I might be able to help.

Unfortunately, after just a few meetings, my emotional health started to suffer. Every time I heard the words "burned to death" I imagined the pain and terror that my parents must have experienced in their final moments. On one occasion, someone handed around photographs of the Stardust venue after the fire had raged through it, and I did not want to touch them, as though the simple black and white images could actually hurt me. I ended up spending most of the meeting close to tears, or actually crying, while the core members of the campaign planned and did their work. I began to have nightmares about the fire, waking up drenched in sweat and sure that I had actually been there myself. My anxiety levels soared, I started to self-harm again, and eventually John advised me to walk away, at least for the time being.

"You're not going to help anyone if you end up having a nervous breakdown," John said. "Chrissie and the others will understand."

I felt very guilty about letting the Keegans down and not playing my part in the campaign, but John was right – at the time, I was barely able to fight for myself, let alone anyone else.

I still feel awful about letting the members of the campaign down all those years ago, because I know how hard they fought for years for justice for the Stardust families. I would like them to know how very grateful I am for all they have done for me, and for all the other survivors and victims of the fire. I know that they have dedicated their lives to this fight for justice, often in the face of studious indifference from our government here in Ireland. So far as I am concerned, they are absolute heroes.

*   *   *

I was desperate to have a child with John, and kept asking him if we could start a family. He said, however, that I was too young to make such a big commitment, and that I might change my mind after going through with it.

"Slow down, love," he said. "we've got all the time in the world."

Even though John was right, and I was indeed very young, I had already started to imagine how wonderful it would be to have his baby. We often took Emma for a day or two to give Alison a break. When little Emma was with us, I could pretend that John, Emma, and I were a family, and envision myself in the role of a mother.

Having Emma for a day or two every so often was wonderful, but it only made me want my own baby even more. I imagined my belly swelling with new life, and how proud and excited I would be to hold a warm, squirming bundle in my arms and know that it was the result of our love for one another. I imagined bringing my new baby to my parents' grave and introducing them, and how I could raise a child with all the love and support in the world and make sure that nothing ever went wrong.

One of the reasons why I had wanted so much to have a relationship with John was to escape from the narrative of the tragic child in which I had been trapped all my life. However, while I gained a lot from our relationship, I found that I was still stuck in that narrative. People always wanted to hear about my experience of growing up without my parents, or to empathise with me about the terrible way in which they had died. Whenever I met a friend of John's for the first time, it was the one thing they wanted to talk about, and I found myself telling the awful story of my parents' death over and over again. I realised that I would never escape, and that I might as well embrace it. I thought that the only true way for me to start over was by making a baby, a new life that would be a clean slate onto which I could inscribe a happy future for us both.

10

Filling the Hole in my Heart

Mam and I planned a big party for my 21st. We rented a function room and invited all our family and friends. I bought a pretty new jumpsuit – black with a lowcut neckline – and gold shoes, and Mam had her hair done; set in tidy blue-rinsed curls, as she always did for special occasions.

"I can't believe it, love," said Mam, her voice full of emotion, as we walked into the function room together. "Time flies. Your daddy would be so proud of you if he could see you today. Look at you now; you're a grown woman and you're gorgeous."

"He *can* see me," I told her, confidently. "I know that they're both looking down from heaven, and thanking you for taking care of me all these years."

"Ah, pet," said Mam, dabbing at her eyes with a handkerchief. "Don't set me off. You know what I'm like. If I start crying, I won't be able to stop!"

The party was a big success. Everyone came, dressed in their finest, and ready to have a few drinks and enjoy the evening. My aunts and uncles were in great form and even Grandad was in a good mood and not getting carried away with the Guinness. He was laughing and joking with everybody. I looked at my family and wished that it could always be like this.

Towards the end of the evening, Mam called John over to her for a chat.

"John," Mam said. "I want you to promise me something."

"What is it?" John asked.

"Will you mind my Lisa?" she asked him. "She doesn't be well. She do suffer something terrible with her anxiety. I'll be gone one of these days, and then she won't have me to lean on anymore, and she'll need all the help she can get."

Mam tapped her two fingers against her temple and looked over at me meaningfully, which was her way of underlining the fact that I sometimes suffered from emotional problems and needed extra support.

Of course, by now John knew me very well, and he had seen how stressed I could get and was already very good at helping me to calm down.

"Of course I will take care of her!" said John. "You can count on me. I'll never let our Lisa down."

"Do you promise?" Mam asked. "I want you to promise. You know how I worry about her. I don't know how she'll manage when I'm gone, and God knows that could be soon, as my lungs are in an awful bad way."

"I promise," said John. "You can rely on me. Lisa will never be alone, so long as I have breath in my body. I'll protect her. You know I'd do anything for her."

"Thanks John," said Mam. "It brings me great comfort to know that you are there for her. I'm very grateful."

The party was wonderful fun. I felt that all my family and friends were there for me and, at least for that evening, I basked in their approval and love and did not feel any of the anxiety that was so often waiting for me around every corner. At last, I thought, the worst of my demons were behind me, and even though I had made plenty of mistakes, I felt confident, that evening, that I could learn from them and get on with the rest of my life.

Two days later, John and I, as well as his daughter Jane, drove down to Mayo to visit his family. As usual, Mary Jane was kind and welcoming, and went to every effort to ensure that I felt perfectly at home. That evening, we went out to a pub in Killala for a few drinks with some of John's family members. When we got home later, John started making a fry-up for Jane and me. I remember sitting there, watching John working in the kitchen, smelling the delicious bacon as it sizzled in the pan, and feeling utterly content in my life, knowing that I had a good man who loved me and who would never let me down. Finally, I thought, my life was as close to perfect as it was ever going to be. At 21, I was beginning to understand how foolish I had been with the money I had been given – effectively throwing so much of it away – but I was also very young and I felt that, with John at my side, I could do anything.

Then John's phone rang, and he fished it out of his pocket to answer it.

"Hello?" said John, and then, "What? *What?* I don't believe you."

John stayed still for a few minutes, nodding gravely as he listened to the speaker on the other end of the line, and then hung up the phone. He came over to me, sat on the sofa beside me, and put his arm around my shoulders. He did not speak to me straight away, just took a long, deep breath to steady his nerves. I could feel his anxiety, and mine started to rise in sympathy with it.

"What is it, John?" I said, feeling my heart and my breathing accelerate. "Is something wrong? What's wrong?"

"Lisa," said John. "Your mam is gone. I'm so sorry."

My whole world retreated into a tunnel of blackness, and I felt sick as I took in John's words while his arm tightened around me. What did he mean? How could she be *gone*? Gone *where*? My mind started scrambling for alternative explanations to what John had said, other than the perfectly obvious one.

"What do you mean, 'gone'?" I asked, my voice rising to a scream. "Where did she go?"

"I'm sorry, love," said John. "She passed away a few minutes ago. She's dead."

I jumped up off the sofa and started to shake and scream.

"It's not true!" I shouted. "She's grand. She has to be grand. Someone's telling you lies. They're just messin'. Who would do something like that? Someone must have a sick sense of humour. It's just a bunch of lies. She'd never leave me without saying goodbye. She loves me! Tell me the truth!"

John tried to hold me, to help me to calm down, but I was having none of it. He assured me that she really was dead, but I just wanted to get back home to see Mam for myself. I did not want to believe that she could really be gone and refused to accept this as the truth, no matter what John said. It was late at night, but I got into the car and demanded that John drive me straight home to Dublin. I cried the whole way there.

When we got back to my grandparents' house, I ran in the front door and straight upstairs to where my grandfather was in bed, on his side and snoring heavily. I started clawing at him, pulling at his nightclothes, and trying to make him sit up so that I could force him to look into my face and provide me with the explanation I demanded.

"What the hell happened to Mam?" I screamed. "Why did nobody help her? Where is she? What happened to her? I go away for the night and you let something go wrong!"

"Sit down, darling," said Grandad. "I didn't do anything to her. I loved her. Sit down and we'll talk about it."

"It's not true!" I shouted at him. "She was absolutely fine the last time I saw her! There was nothing wrong with her at all!"

"Calm down," Grandad said. "Come on now, calm down."

"I won't calm down!" I yelled. I started pulling at the vest Grandad was wearing. "I want some answers, and I want them now! She's not supposed to be dead. This is not right, for fuck's sake."

"Jesus, love," said Grandad. "Get a hold of yourself. You're losing the plot. We've got to be strong for one another now."

Eventually I calmed down enough to go downstairs. Grandad followed me down and we sat at the kitchen table. When I saw him under the electric light, I could see how pale, shocked and upset he was. He had just lost the love of his life. I screamed and cried until the sun rose while Grandad tried, ineffectually, to comfort me and to explain that there was nothing anyone could have done to save Mam. She had not been well for some time, and her heart had been under enormous pressure. Grandad said that we should take comfort from the fact that she had died suddenly, and had not suffered. I knew that he was right, but I still could not – and would not – accept that Mam had died, and nobody was to blame. That it was just the natural order of things.

Eventually, I was calm enough to listen to Alison's account of what had happened.

Alison and Mam had come home the evening before, just at the time when John and I were having a nice time in the pub in Killala. The central heating was on in the house, and it was very warm.

"Jesus, love," said Mam to Alison when they came in the front door together. "It's awful hot."

Mam started pulling at her coat to remove it as she walked towards the kitchen, where no doubt she planned to sit in her usual seat, with its view of my father's photograph. She had only gone a few steps when she fell over and landed heavily on the floor. Alison rushed over to help her up, but Mam literally was dead before she hit the ground. Poor Alison was left all alone to ring an ambulance and tell the family what had happened. I cannot even imagine how she dealt with the stress.

In the morning, John and I went home to get ready for the funeral, which was going to be held the following day; Mam's body was already with the undertaker. I had stopped crying, but I felt numb and empty with grief and I still struggled to accept what had happened. Back at the house, I tried to think carefully about what to wear for the funeral, because I knew that Mam had always liked to see me looking nice – but nothing seemed to matter anymore. Eventually I put on a sombre black suit that reflected my mood.

Mam's wake was at Jenning's Funeral Home on Seville Place, just a few yards away from where her old house had once stood. Her hair was still beautifully set from my 21st party and she wore the same dress that she had worn that evening; the undertaker had very little work to do to get her ready for her open coffin. Eventually, after everyone had said their goodbyes and kissed her for the last time, it was time for the undertaker to put the lid on the coffin. I clung to John's arm as the heavy wooden lid obscured Mam's beloved face.

The funeral Mass was held in the Church of Our Lady of Lourdes on Séan MacDermott Street – the church that Mam had attended as a child – and we had a reception at Lloyd's pub on Amiens Street, where she had always loved to go for a drink or two with her lady friends. Hundreds of people came – all of our old neighbours and friends from the Sheriff Street area, and everyone whose lives she had touched along the way.

I do not think that Mam ever realised quite how popular she was, or how many people knew her and appreciated the role that she had played in their lives. Mam had been such a warm, loving woman that everyone she met liked and respected her, and she had been a cherished member of the Sheriff Street community for most of her adult life.

I was proud to see how many people had come to the funeral, but I was still in a state of shock, and I have only a patchy memory of the events of that day. I know that John was at my side all day long and that he held me and helped me to stay sane.

After the funeral Mass, we buried Mam in the same grave as my dad – her beloved boy, Francis – at the graveyard in Sutton, as was her wish. She had often said that when she died, at least she would be near her son. This thought had often brought her some comfort. As we stood at her grave-side, hundreds of people must have shaken my hand and told me that they were sorry for my trouble. Of those hundreds, scores mentioned the fact that Mam had taken me in and raised me after the Stardust fire, and they commented on how lucky I had been to have a woman like her in my life. I knew that day that I would never stop missing her, and I never have. Not a day goes by when I do not think of her.

I will never forget how I felt on the day of Mam's funeral. I had lived all my life with the knowledge that I was already bereaved – but I had no conscious memory of my parents, and this was the first time that I had actually lost someone close to me since Maureen and Francis were killed. I remember thinking that, even though I was only 21 years old, I would never say the word "Mam" again, and that if – God willing – I had children of my own one day, they would have no grandmother to play with them and tell them stories about the past. With Mam gone, I also felt that another thread connecting me to my parents had been severed, and that they were drifting even further away from me.

When Mam died, she took a little part of me with her. I still miss her every day, and I always will. The one thing that brings me comfort when I think of her is the belief that she was reunited with Francis in heaven, and that, together, they are still looking down on me and helping me to make the right decisions as I continue on my journey through life.

Grandad was a diminished man after his wife's death in every way: physically, because without Mam's delicious cooking, he lost weight and became smaller and a less imposing presence, and emotionally, because he seemed to have very little fight left in him. It was sad to watch him changing and declining so quickly, and it was clear that he was not well at all. I often found him sitting, all alone, in the front room of the house in Marino, crying. It was a big change from before, when he had been more likely to roar and shout and to demand that everyone paid him attention and gave him the respect that he felt he was due as the man of the house.

I knew that Grandad missed his beloved wife, and I did feel sorry for him – but part of me wondered if he was really crying out of a sense of guilt, because he knew that the heavy drink-ing, the roaring, and the screaming, had been more than Mam could cope with, and had contributed to her sudden death. Sometimes these thoughts overwhelmed me. I found it difficult to sleep and my decision-making abilities were impacted by the high levels of anxiety I experienced. John was worried about me, and begged me to get some help before my mental health was seriously impacted.

I went to my GP and explained my situation to her, and she prescribed some anti-anxiety medication that would help to take the edge off the symptoms. I was thankful for the help but, although I did not fully accept it at the time, I knew that I had deeper issues that would need to be resolved in order for my anxiety to reduce to a manageable level. Still, in retro-spect I can see that this visit to the GP was the first modest step I took towards gaining control over my own situation and accepting that I could not continue to go through life without taking responsibility for my own happiness.

*   *   *

When I was 22, and just beginning to deal with my emotional issues, a miracle happened. Alison was still living with Grandad, and she was in the house one day when I popped in for a visit. She was in the living room taking care of Emma – who was a wonderful little girl now and an absolute credit to her mother. Alison was also taking care of a baby I had never met before. The baby, a little boy, was crawling on the floor and looking curiously at everything around him. He looked up at me as I walked in. He was an absolutely beautiful child with dark slanted eyes, a mop of shiny dark hair, and a big smile.

"Jesus, Alison," I said. "Who owns that baby? He's only gorgeous."

I picked up the baby and hugged him. He snuggled against my shoulder and buried his little face in my neck. I could feel his hot breath against my skin.

"Aww," I said delightedly. "He likes me! Look at him! What a perfect child."

Alison explained that a friend of hers was the mother of the baby and that she had asked Alison to take care of him for a while because she was unwell.

"His name is Craig," Alison said. "His dad is Chinese; that's why he's got those eyes. He's gorgeous, isn't he?"

"God, he's so beautiful," I said. "He's just the ideal little child, isn't he?"

"Yeah…" Alison's voice tailed off.

Something in the slur of Alison's words made me look at her sharply, and I realised that she was on heroin and not completely all there. She was not utterly out of it, but she should not have been on her own looking after Emma and this lovely little baby. I spent the afternoon with Alison, helping out, until she was better.

The next day, Alison introduced me to her friend, Craig's mother. The other woman was clearly very unwell, and I could see that she was not in a position to take care of her child. I asked her if there was anything I could do to help.

"D'you want me to mind him for you?" I asked. "It'd be no bother at all. I'd be delighted."

"Okay," she said. "Come down to my house on Friday and you can take him with you and let him stay with you for a while. Thanks."

I picked up Craig that Friday and drove home with him buckled into Emma's old car seat. He smiled at me all the way back. As soon as I got into the apartment, I rang John.

"You should see this little baby," I said to John. "He's so beautiful, and his mammy says that I can mind him for a while because she's not well."

When John came home, he agreed that Craig was a beautiful child, but he had some concerns about me taking care of another woman's child.

"Lisa, don't start this," John said. "Who owns that baby? Tell me the truth, now."

"Relax," I told him. "His mother is a friend of mine and Alison's. She knows he's with me. This is all completely above board. I'm just doing this lady a favour because she's not well and needs a bit of help. What do you think – that I'd take someone's baby on the street?"

John looked a bit shame-faced.

"Sorry, Lisa," he said. "I know you'd never steal someone's baby; I know you've a big heart."

Four weeks later, Craig's mother was still unable to take care of him and John and I had fallen completely in love with this little boy.

Craig was the perfect child. He was 17 months old – the same age that I had been when my parents died. I felt that I could empathise with him because, even though I could not remember it, I had been through the same experience of being separated from my parents. Craig often cried and every time the door opened he looked straight at it and his little face lit up. I knew that he was hoping that his mother would come in and that even though she was not currently in his life, he loved her.

I wanted to keep Craig, but I was afraid I would get into trouble for doing so without official documentation to give me the right to be his guardian, so after Craig had been with me for a month, I brought him around to his grandmother's house to see what the family wanted to do about his care.

"His mam is not here," Craig's grandmother said. "She'll be here this evening. I can't cope with a baby right now. We have plenty to be dealing with in this family at the moment. Can't you keep him for now? I can see that he likes you."

"I'd be delighted!" I said, and ran off with Craig before his grandmother could change her mind.

"Jesus, Lisa," John fretted, when another week or so had gone by. "You'd better tell the authorities that we have him. We can't just keep someone else's child indefinitely. Surely that would be kidnapping? Like, what's the plan here? Keep him until he's a grown man or what? Eventually someone will notice that he's not ours, and we could get into trouble."

"Okay," I said. "I'll tell the guards and hopefully they can tell me what to do."

I went down to the local garda station at Whitehall, and walked up to the desk with little Craig in my arms.

"Listen," I said to the officer on duty, "I was minding this baby for a girl I know, and she's not well and she can't take him back. His granny can't mind him either. What do you think I should do with him? I'm happy to keep him, but is there somebody I'm supposed to tell about it?"

"Oh, Jesus," said the officer. "I don't know. Try the granny again and come back to me if you've any problems. But if you're minding him with their permission, then I suppose everything is okay."

I brought Craig back to his grandmother's house and knocked on the door once again. I was secretly hoping that Craig's mother's family would not want him back yet, but his grandmother took him from me and said that she would return him to his mother. Bereft, I went back home and fell into John's arms, sobbing.

"I can't believe she took him back!" I wept. "I thought that maybe they would let me keep him a bit longer. I'm going to miss him so much. I just love Craig to pieces. I couldn't love him more if he were my own."

"There's nothing we could have done, Lisa," said John, comforting me. "It's only right that Craig should be with his family. At least you had him for a little while and I am sure that they appreciated your help."

"I don't know, John," I fretted. "Craig's family seem to have a lot of troubles, and I think he was happy with us. What if they can't take care of him properly?"

A few days after dropping Craig back to his family home, I had to attend a funeral of another friend of Alison's – a lovely young woman and another casualty of the heroin epidemic. After the funeral, I was in my car and about to drive home when I saw Craig's mother gesticulating on the street. For a minute, I thought she was playing with some children, but then I realised that she was beckoning to me. I drove up to her and wound down the window.

"What's wrong?" I asked. "Are you all right?"

"The social services are after taking my Craig, Lisa," she said. I noticed that her eyes were bloodshot and that she had been crying. "I don't know where they are going to put him, but he's at the hospital now. Can you help me? We need to get there fast. The poor little baby."

My stomach lurched. How could this have happened, when I had just brought Craig home a couple of days before?

"What's going on?" I asked. "Why did they take him?"

"I don't know," she said. "They just did."

"Get into the car," I told her. "We'll go up to the hospital together."

Before I could drive on, my phone started ringing. I answered the phone and a woman's voice introduced herself as a social worker. She explained that Craig's mother had given her my number, and asked me if I had been taking care of him recently. I said that I had, and asked what was going on.

"Craig has been taken into protective custody," the social worker said. "Can you come to Temple Street Hospital straight away to talk to me?"

"Oh God," I said. "Of course I can. I'll do whatever I can to help."

I hung up and told Craig's mother about the social worker's call. She was still very upset, and we agreed that we would go to the hospital together.

"The social workers don't believe me," she said, "but I really do love that baby with all my heart."

I rang John and told him to come to Temple Street straight away, because Craig was in trouble. Then, hanging up, I sped up the road and went straight to the hospital. Craig's mother cried the whole way. When we got there, the social worker explained that Craig had been left alone in his mother's house and had crawled out into the garden, where he stuck a rusty coat hanger in his eye. The neighbours had phoned the guards when they heard his screams. The guards arrived within minutes, knocked the door down, and found Craig wailing in the back yard with the hanger still dangling from his eye and blood pouring down his lovely little face.

"Listen," the social worker said to me. "Would you be able to take Craig for the weekend until we find a foster home for him? He already knows you, and we don't want to cause him any more stress than necessary. Craig's grandmother says that you have a good bond with him, and it would be good for him to be with someone he knows and trusts. I am sure it would be a relief to his mother and grandmother to know that he is with someone who already knows him and cares about him."

"I'll do more than that," I said. "If it's okay with his mother, I'll take him for good. I'm keeping him as long as he needs me. He has a home with me."

That very day, Craig's mother signed her baby into voluntary care and I became his foster mother. I am sure that this was very difficult for her, and I know that she loved Craig, but the simple fact is that she was not well enough to take care of him at the time.

"Take care of him for me," she said. "He's the joy of my heart."

"I will," I said. "And I'll make sure he never forgets you."

Craig's mother and I hugged one another and she walked back out onto the street. I only ever saw her again in the distance. She has had a tough life, and I respect her for having made such a difficult decision at a time when she was really near rock bottom.

As his mother left, Craig raised his fat little arms to me, asking to be picked up. I lifted him and pressed him into me, whispering reassuring words in his ear. I could feel his tiny heart beating quickly against mine, and although the situation was heart-breaking in many ways, I felt a little shoot of pure joy sprout in my soul.

That was the moment when I became a mother, the day my life started again and I began to heal. That was the moment when I realised that I could be truly happy.

John and I strapped baby Craig into the car seat that we had bought for him while he was staying with us, and drove him home. We stopped at a Tesco on the way and filled a shopping cart with Pampers, baby powder, formula, baby food and everything that Craig would need. We were so excited and happy; we were like two children on Christmas Day. God knows what little Craig was thinking, but he kept showing me his dimples and asking to be picked up.

When people think about children who are taken into care, they usually imagine the story from the child's point of view – how they are saved from difficult circumstances, and all the trauma they suffer. When I think of how Craig came into my life, all I can see is how he saved me. Craig gave meaning and purpose to my life. He gave me a reason not just to live, but to do what was necessary to start confronting my demons and finally finish growing up. I know, without a shadow of a doubt, that Craig's presence in my life is the result of my parents' help. I know that they heard my desperate prayers at their gravesides, and I am confident that, somehow, they were able to intervene to save both Craig and me.

I could see that there were a lot of parallels between Craig's situation, and the situation I had been in at the same age. His mother was still alive, but she was not able to care for him. My parents had both been killed. Before we could even talk, both Craig and I had been taken out of the only environment we had ever known, and sent to live with someone else.

While Craig was an absolutely delightful baby, I am sure that he was puzzled and confused by everything that had happened. I am sure that he often looked at me, when I bent over him in his cot, and wondered where his mother had gone and why I had taken her place. In the early months of his time with John and me, Craig cried a lot. My heart broke for him, because I knew that he must miss his mother terribly and also because I knew that I had been through the same thing myself. I promised Craig that I would do whatever I could to ensure that he would have a happy childhood.

Instinctively, I felt that the best way to take care of Craig was to keep him with me all the time and to make sure that he knew that he was loved. I remembered my own childhood, when I had often felt very insecure about how people felt towards me, despite Mam's great love for me and the huge effort she had gone to, to raise me. I did not want Craig to ever wonder about my feelings for him but, instead, to be sure of my unconditional love.

Craig slept with me every night; his little warm body snuggled up against mine. My face was the last thing he saw every night before going to sleep, and the first thing he saw every morning. When I walked around the house, I carried him in my arms. He came with me to the hairdresser, the supermarket, the beauty parlour. We were never apart.

John and I could not have loved Craig more if we had made him ourselves, and at long last I began to experience some positive feelings towards myself. I had not self-harmed for some time, even though I had often thought about doing so. I knew from experience that cutting myself was the one thing that brought me a sense of relief when everything just seemed to be too much. When Craig came into my life, all of my bad thoughts about myself just went away, like snow melting on a summer's day, along with any desire to hurt myself.

I understand now that the negative emotions and actions I had lived with before had sprung from the feeling that I was worthless. When Craig looked at me with his big smile, buried his little head in my neck, or reached his little arms up towards me to be picked up, I knew that I was not worthless at all, because I meant the world to him.

Not long after Craig was put into my custody, I got a phone call from Alison one day while I was caring for Emma. I often took Emma for a day or two to give Alison a break.

"Could you come down to the house and bring Emma?" Alison asked. "There's a social worker here, and she wants to check in on Emma and make sure that she's doing okay."

Alison had moved into her own place and was doing her absolute best with Emma, even though she had not managed to come off the drugs and was still taking both street drugs and the methadone prescribed by the clinic. Even so, my heart started racing, because I was sure that the social worker would want to take Emma away from Alison and place her in protective custody. I had already seen how quickly the social services had acted to take Craig away from his mother when they felt that he was not safe with her.

I gathered up Emma and her things and went to Alison's as quickly as I could. I was already planning to offer to take

Emma and raise her myself as Craig's older sister, if it meant that she wouldn't be taken into care. I could not bear the thought of her being taken away to be raised by people we did not know.

Thankfully, today was a good day. Alison was not on the drugs – or at least not obviously so – and Emma was very clearly a well-cared-for, happy little girl. The social worker was kind and pleasant, and just wanted to make sure everything was all right. In fact, she said that Emma was doing very well, and that Alison was a good mother. I felt very proud of them both and, when the social worker left, Alison and I waved goodbye to her with a huge feeling of relief.

One of the first things I needed to do as a mother was to make sense of some of the things that I had gone through as a child and teenager. I felt that I needed closure and some explanations, so that I could move on and be the best mother to Craig that I could possibly be. I had never really discussed with anyone the sexual abuse I had suffered at the hands of another girl when I was a small child. I did understand that she had also been a child at the time – albeit five years older than me, which had seemed like a lot then – and that there may have been mitigating circumstances that led her to behave the way she did, but I still wanted to hear her apology.

The first time I raised the issue with her, I rang her up and put the phone on loudspeaker because I had a friend with me and I wanted her to hear the conversation and to know that my stories about the abuse were true.

My former abuser was contrite and sounded genuinely sorry for what she had done.

"I'm real sorry I abused you, Lisa," she said. "I didn't know what I was doing. But it's all water under the bridge, right?"

It meant a lot to me to hear her admitting what she had done, and also to know that my friend had heard her, too. I hated the thought of telling people what had happened, and not being believed.

But shortly afterwards, when I saw her in person on the street, she was furious with me. She did not want anyone to know what had happened years ago, when we were kids. She went into a rage and beat me so badly that I ended up at the garda station, my face covered in blood, reporting her for assault. I could barely make the report because I was crying so hard.

As a child, I had never once cried when I was abused. I had been still and silent, praying for it to end and hoping that it would just go away. Now it was as though something had opened up inside me and all my childhood pain welled up and out in the form of huge, wrenching sobs.

Eventually I managed to make the report, and the police conducted some interviews, but it was all so long ago that they were unable to put together a case. I realised that if I wanted real healing and retribution, I would have to find it inside myself, because it was never going to come from anybody else.

11

Hellos and Goodbyes

All my life, even in my happiest times, my heart had always felt a little bit broken. Craig helped me to start feeling whole again and I devoted myself to him. Craig was a dream child – sweet-natured, quiet, and placid. While he had cried a lot in the early days, he seemed much more confident now. When Craig started to talk, he called me "Lisa" at first. That was fine with me – it was just wonderful to see him reaching his milestones and doing so well. I felt that I was Craig's mother, but I knew and understood that he had his own story to tell and that I could not force him or anyone else to see me that way.

Then, one day, Craig woke up, held up his arms to me to be picked up, and said "Up, Mam!" Shortly after that, he started calling John "Dad." We were very excited, and felt proud and honoured that Craig saw us as his parents. John had been sure that he did not want or need more children than the four he had already, but he could not have been prouder of Craig. We both were. Craig soon became the sun around whom our lives revolved.

Taking care of Craig was such a pleasure that I loved sharing him with all the people I cared about. John's daughter Jane had left school by now and was training to be a hairdresser at a salon in the city centre. I used to take Craig into town so that we could all meet when Jane was taking a break from work.

"That young fella will think he lives in the hairdresser!" said John. "Who are you trying to turn him into, Vidal Sassoon?"

I always dressed Craig up in gorgeous little outfits to go into the city centre, and loved it when strangers stopped to comment on what a cute child he was. Jane and all her friends from the hairdresser's loved him, and he would get passed from one girl to the next as they all took pictures of him and admired his clothes and his sweet, smiling nature.

When Craig was little, I tried to stay in touch with his birth mother and her family. This is what the social workers recommended, and as someone who had not grown up with her biological parents, I could see that maintaining a line of contact was the ideal. Despite my strong feelings for Craig, I was only his foster mother, which meant that if things got better for his biological mother, he might go back to live with her one day. But Craig's biological mother was still very unwell and unfortunately she did not get better as time passed. I can only imagine how difficult it was for her to see her little boy being raised by someone else. I respected her for having made this difficult decision, and for sticking to it, because I could see that the best way for her to show her love for her son was to acknowledge that she was not able to take care of him. Gradually, however, it became more difficult to stay in touch, and the contact tapered off.

At this time, I met a wonderful woman of about my own age, Liz. We hit it off immediately and became close friends. From the start, I knew I could depend on Liz. She was a fantastic support to me as I cared for little Craig, and I often visited Liz and her mother to show off his latest achievements. Liz's own children were slightly older than Craig, and they played with him nicely while we drank tea and chatted.

On Sundays, Liz and I – and often her partner and John, too – met up for a meal and sometimes a quick dance at a nightclub. I was increasingly proud of myself for having a normal life with a beautiful child, supportive friends, and an active and wholesome social life. I had moved past the dark days of my earlier years and was happy in my present and looking forward to the future.

Sometimes John and I put Craig in his little car seat and brought him down to Mayo to visit John's family: his mother, Mary Jane, his sister Mary, and his brothers Jimmy and Frank. They all warmly welcomed Craig into their extended family. John was still a country man at heart, and he needed his little breaks in the green landscape of Mayo. Craig loved it there, and John used to let him run wild in the fields near Mary Jane's house. As I was such a city girl, I was always scared that Craig might get run over by a sheep or fall into a rabbit-hole. I had no idea about the countryside and imagined it as being full of hazards that a Dubliner like me would never understand. I would stand in the window of the house and watch out anxiously the whole time. Craig was so small that sometimes the grass, or the occasional bunch of reeds, was taller than he was, and my heart would lurch when Craig's little dark head disappeared behind the greenery.

"Be careful, John!" I would call out. "Don't let him hurt himself. I'm keeping my eye on you!"

John would just wave and pretend he couldn't hear me, because he knew how to take care of a small child – in fact, having raised four of them, he could reasonably claim to know a lot more about it than me. For John, the beautiful landscape of Mayo was not a dangerous place at all, but the bucolic rural environment in which he had had such a happy childhood. Naturally, he wanted to share his love of the countryside with Craig.

"Ah God," I would say to John's mother. "He's not paying me any attention at all! He's just letting the child do whatever he wants!"

"Well, isn't that a good thing, *a stór?*" she said. "It gives you time to have a cup of tea and put your feet up. Leave John with the little lad and I'll put the kettle on and make us both a nice cup of tea."

When Craig was about three, I signed him up for a local playgroup because I felt that he would benefit from spending more time with other young children. The caregiver was a wonderful woman called Lisa Connolly. Craig became friendly with Lisa's son and absolutely adored his time at the playgroup. He thrived, and continued to learn and grow. His placid nature made it easy for him to make friends, and I was so happy to see him smile when I dropped him off.

When the time came for Craig to go to primary school, I enrolled him in a lovely school in Ballyboughal, a village in north County Dublin where John had a house – we all moved into the house and settled there for a time. I was so proud when Craig started school, and just thrilled and excited to see him in his school uniform. He was happy in school, and got along well with both the teachers and the students. I could not help comparing his experience with mine at the same age. For me, despite the kindness of the teachers, school had been a place of fear and pain. For Craig, it was completely different. He would just wave goodbye to me and run into school, delighted to know that he was going to spend the day with his little friends. As he grew up, I could see his personality developing and enjoyed seeing him become progressively more confident with other people.

I did not need to visit my parents' grave as often as before, but I did talk to Craig occasionally about his granny and grandad in heaven. Once in a while we visited their graves to bring them flowers and say a little prayer together for the safe repose of their souls. When Craig could talk, he said he wanted to see my parents, and I had to explain that they were gone, and that they were never coming back. I realised that he had thought that they actually lived underground, and that if we asked nicely, they might come out to have a cup of tea with us. Probably, I thought, I had imagined something similar when I was his age, although I did not remember it. Perhaps that is where I got the idea – which I never completely shed until I was well into my teens – that my mother might come back one day.

* * *

All through my teenage years, I had worried and fretted about Alison and Denis because they were taking so much heroin, and I knew that they could easily take an overdose and die, or just get so sick that they wasted away. I worried most about Alison, largely because we were so close, and I could not imagine life without her. Alison had told me that she had had heart palpitations a few times, and that she was worried that her heart had been damaged by years of unhealthy behaviour. I told her that I was sure her heart would get better if she came off the drugs that she craved so much, but she just shrugged and changed the subject.

My relationship with Alison was difficult sometimes. I loved her, and she loved me, but I was often very frustrated by the fact that she did not seem to even try to come off the drugs. She was always asking me to lend her money, as her benefits were not enough to maintain her habit. Denis was not well either and, for Craig's sake, I limited contact with my family at this time. I loved them all, but I did not want Craig to grow up accepting a drug addict's behaviour as normal. I wanted him to have positive role models who would show him a good, healthy way to live, and I was very aware that I was responsible for keeping him out of harm's way.

One day, I was in the hairdresser having my highlights put in when I got a call from Auntie Mary.

"You'd better get yourself to the Mater Hospital," she said, getting straight to the point. "Denis is dead."

"Ah no, ah Jesus," I said. "What the fuck happened?"

Auntie Mary just sighed.

"Come to the hospital, and everything will be explained to you," she said.

I had to pull the tinfoil out of my hair and rush to the hospital with my hair still full of product and tied back to keep it out of my face.

Adrian had found Denis in a cold, wet laneway off Dorset Street in Dublin's inner city the night before. He had been unconscious and Adrian could not rouse him. Immediately alarmed, Adrian picked Denis up, threw him over his shoulder, and carried him to the Mater Private Hospital, which is located in that area.

Even though Denis was not a private patient, the doctors at the Mater Private tried to treat him. When he failed to respond, Denis was transferred to the Mater Public, where he was pronounced dead after 20 minutes. I think that Denis had probably already been dead when Adrian found him, and I can only imagine how traumatic this must have been for him, especially because he and Denis had always been close. Denis was just 43 years old and should have been in the prime of his life.

Denis had a small funeral and was buried in the family plot in Sutton, above my dad and Mam. I remember standing at the edge of the grave, crying while John tried to comfort me. I was desperately sad that Denis was gone, but also angry with him for throwing his beautiful life away. He had been such a lovely young man, with so much potential, and when I was a child he had been one of the most positive people in my life. At any point over the past two decades, since Denis had started taking the drugs, he could have turned his life around. Instead, he had allowed his addiction to rule his life, and now his children were going to grow up without a father, and the rest of us would have to live on with our anger and our grief.

My father had left me through no choice of his own – the Stardust fire had ended his life. But Denis, who was one of the most intelligent men I had known growing up, could have chosen to live. Instead, he had allowed heroin to gain complete control over him. I believe that Denis never really recovered from the loss of his brother Francis, especially because his parents had been too distraught to give him the help he needed at the time, because they were busy with their own grief – and with me.

By the time Denis died, he had looked like the sort of man most people would cross the street to avoid. Think of how harshly most people talk about the addicted: they call them junkies, zombies and scum, and sometimes even joke about how the world would be a better place if they were all dead. They are talking about people like Denis. Denis had given in to petty crime to fund his addiction, and he spent most of his time on the streets and was frequently in trouble with the police. But I knew that inside that broken man, there was a lovely, smiling, kind person who could have been so much more. Now Denis was just a statistic: yet another person from the north inner city whose life had been stolen by addiction.

His funeral was a heart-breaking affair, not least because so many of Denis's friends in attendance were themselves addicts, and were probably wondering which one of them would go next. His friends were an assembly of the walking dead.

People who have never had a family member or close friend with a heroin addiction often find it very easy to dismiss addicts. They see them lurching around the city, completely out of it, and they turn away from them in disgust. Do not get me wrong: I know where that reaction comes from. The thing is, though, that addicts do not start out like that. A lot of very nice people get caught up in drug-taking. Many of them manage to get out of it before their lives go completely off-track, but not all of them do. For those who love them, watching an addict's health and sense of self steadily decline is absolutely heart-breaking.

*   *   *

Grandad was on holiday when he started feeling unwell, so he was brought home and sent straight to hospital. When the doctors examined him, they quickly found out that he was riddled with cancer, and that he had very little time left to live. The cancer was everywhere, including in his brain. This may be one of the factors that contributed to the change in his behaviour and loss of impulse control in the last few years of his life. If only it had been diagnosed earlier, a lot of heartbreak could have been avoided.

After a week in hospital, Grandad was allowed to go home to spend his remaining months surrounded by his family. We made up a bed for Grandad in the downstairs bedroom, so that he could rest while still taking part in family life as much as possible. His health continued to decline, and so did his cognitive state. I hoped that there would be time for Grandad to accept that he had not always been very kind to me, and that he would give me the opportunity to forgive him, but it seemed as though time was running out. My feelings towards Grandad at this time were very complex. I loved him, and knew that he loved me, and I wondered how things had gone so badly wrong during my teenage years.

When he was readmitted to the Mater Hospital for a week, Grandad was upset and confused, and kept begging us not to leave him there. He regressed to his childhood and asked us to promise that he would not be sent to Cork Street – when Grandad was a little boy, there had been a fever hospital on Cork Street that Dubliners regarded with dread, as it had the reputation of being a place where people were sent to die.

One day, I went to visit Grandad in the hospital, and he fished €20 out of the pocket of his pyjamas and asked me to fetch him two pints of Guinness from the nurses' station. I realised that he thought that he was in the pub.

"Grandad!" I said, "you're in hospital, you mad yoke! There's no pints in here."

"Not at all," Grandad said. "I've been drinkin' in here for hours. There was killin's in here last night, and I had to sort out a bit of trouble."

Upsetting as the situation was, I could only laugh. I was glad that Grandad thought that he was in the pub, because at least he was enjoying himself.

On other occasions, Grandad would be disoriented and upset. He would toss and turn so much in his bed that his nightclothes and sheets got tangled around his body. I would lean in and try to untangle them and he would get confused. Thinking that I was a nurse, he would tell me quite crossly to have a word with the woman who was poking him and get her to stop. Sometimes he talked about Denis, who had died just a few weeks before, and said that he was the first of his children to die and that it was an awful thing, to be an old man and see your children go before you. I would remind him that Francis, my dad, had died too, over 20 years before, but Grandad seemed only to remember the last few months of his life with any degree of clarity. I felt hurt that my father seemed to have been erased from Grandad's memory, but it was not his fault.

After a week, the hospital allowed Grandad to go back home again. As soon as he was out of the hospital bed and in his own clothes, he asked us to take him to the pub. We reasoned that as he was dying anyway, he might as well get his wish, so we took him out for a pint. That pint turned out to be his last. When he had finished it, we brought him home, where a nurse from the local hospice was on hand to help his family nurse him and provide him with palliative care.

In his final days, while he was dying, Grandad kept asking me to hug him. The day before he died, he summoned me and told me that he was leaving his estate to be divided between his children, and that he had set aside €10,000 for me. I know that, in his own way, he was asking for forgiveness for the emotional torture I had suffered at his hands as a teenage girl and young woman. I told him that everything was right between us, because I didn't want him facing death with his regrets hanging over him.

My Uncle Don was in Mountjoy jail during Grandad's final days, serving time for acting as the get-away driver during a post office robbery, but he was given compassionate leave to visit his father. A nun who worked with the prison accompanied Don home, so that he could say goodbye to Grandad. She was very sweet, and she sat and drank tea in the kitchen while Don sat with Grandad, holding his hand. We all watched Don anxiously during the visit because we were afraid that he would use the opportunity to escape. When he had said goodbye to Don, Grandad seemed to feel that he could go now, as he had made his peace with all of us.

When he went into his final agony, Grandad started shaking furiously and his death rattle began; it was painfully difficult to observe. The local priest came to the house to provide the last rites, which was something of a comfort. Grandad passed after that, and the local GP came and pronounced him dead. Two days later, Grandad joined Francis, Denis and Mam in the family plot.

I was sad when Grandad passed, although not nearly as grief-stricken I had been at my grandmother's funeral. Most of all, I was sad for him, because of all the opportunities he had wasted during his time on earth and for the various ways in which he had hurt both me and other people in his life. Grandad had many good qualities – I had never doubted his love for Mam, and he had been a very hard worker who had supported a large, demanding family. For whatever reason, however, he had embraced the darkness inside him and had, too often, given himself over to anger, bitterness and shame. It had been an awful waste and I wish that things had been different.

I remember looking at Alison on the day of Grandad's funeral. Poor Alison had been physically as well as mentally transformed by her addiction. Most of her teeth were gone, her cheeks were sunken, and she was hardly recognisable as the pretty young woman she had been just a few years earlier. On the day of Grandad's funeral, she looked pale and exhausted. We were all upset, obviously, but Alison did not look well at all.

"Are you okay, Alison?" I asked. "You're awful pale."

"I've a terrible bad pain in my side," she said. "I've had it for a few days, and it won't go away. I've been taking things for it, but nothing seems to make any difference."

"Jesus, Alison," I said. "You'd better see someone about that. It could be serious. You need to mind yourself; you need to stay well for Emma."

"I'm going to the clinic tomorrow," Alison said. "I'll have a word with the doctor then."

Alison visited the methadone clinic regularly, and the doctors kept an eye on her general health. At the clinic, the doctor suggested that she have a full health check, including a series of blood tests.

"I don't need one of them!" Alison said. "I take care of myself! I'm a mother, you know. I know I need to stay well for my daughter."

Alison was very indignant, because she assumed that the doctor thought she didn't take basic precautions with her health, or that she did not understand how important it was for her to stay alive so that she could take care of Emma.

"Well, I'll give you one anyway," the doctor said. "Just to check. Maybe there's no cause for concern, but it's better to be safe than sorry, right?"

The doctor drew some of Alison's blood and sent it away to be tested. A few days later, the clinic rang Alison and asked her to come back in for a second test. She knew what this meant, because if the test showed that there was nothing wrong, the clinic only rang once to share the good news, to stop the patient worrying. If it was bad news, they asked them to come in for a second test so that they would not get too upset and do something rash while they were on their own. The clinic doctors would then break the bad news to them in person.

When she went back to the clinic, the doctor said that Alison's health was very bad and that her organs were starting to fail. The doctor explained to Alison that many people could live long and fairly healthy lives even after having damaged their health through addiction, especially if they got off the drugs, stayed off them, and led a good lifestyle.

"Look on this as a wake-up call," the doctor said kindly. "Maybe this is what you need to realise that you just have to come off the drugs and take care of yourself, so that you'll get better and be there for your daughter. That's what you want, isn't it?"

But the bad news devastated Alison, and she lost the will to live. Up until then, while she never managed to come off the drugs, she had tried to keep her life more or less on track, so that she could take care of Emma, who was the light of her life. Now, she felt that she had a death sentence hanging over her and she gave up.

We were all very worried about Alison, but increasingly her behaviour pushed people away. All I could do for her now was help with Emma whenever I could. Emma was just heading into her teenage years, and she needed a lot of support.

One day, Alison phoned. As soon as I heard her voice, I registered the note of urgency in it.

Here we go again, I thought. *She needs money for drugs.*

"What do you want this time?" I asked Alison, rather curtly. "Or should I say, 'how much'?"

"What?" said Alison. "No, it's not money. Listen, Lisa, I need to ask you something important, and I want you to listen carefully."

"What is it?"

I was very struck by her serious tone of voice.

"If anything ever happens to me, will you mind my Emma? I want you to promise. She's the apple of my eye, and I need to know that someone will be there for her when I'm gone."

"What are you talking about?" I chided her. "Nothing is going to happen to you. You're only a young woman. You just need to take care of yourself a bit more. You'll be here for a long time yet, minding Emma yourself."

"Just promise," Alison insisted. "Please? It would mean an awful lot to me."

"Okay," I said. "I promise. But Alison, we'll be old ladies together. I'll be right there beside you when Emma gets married, and when she makes you a granny."

Alison died of an overdose three weeks later. One of our cousins, who was living with her at the time, came home to find her collapsed in the living room of her flat. He tried to rouse her, and called the ambulance when she did not wake up. By the time the medics had arrived, it was too late – Alison was gone.

Alison had taken so many different pills, and ingested so many different drugs, including both methadone from the clinic and heroin from the street, that her death could not be attributed to just one of them. Fortunately, Emma – who was 13 at the time – had gone to the seaside that day with some friends, and did not see her mother dying or dead. She was brought back to my Aunt Mary's house, and when she walked in, she saw the whole family gathered together.

"What is it?" Emma asked. "Is Mammy dead?"

Nobody answered, but we all burst into tears. Emma went into hysterics and had to be held until she stopped crying. It was heart-breaking.

"You know you have us," I said. "I'll never let you down."

The rest of the family said similar things. We all wanted Emma to know that we loved her and would do our best to help her to finish growing up now that her mother was gone.

The doctor who performed Alison's inquest said that he had no idea how Alison had managed to survive as long as she did, because her internal organs were falling apart. If she had made some changes to her lifestyle after her medical check, she might have been able to pull herself back from the brink, but instead she had given up. She was just 37 years old. I was devastated – the whole family was. Nobody was more devastated than Emma, who had just lost her mother. I felt absolutely heartbroken for her, because I knew what it was like.

12

Fresh Starts

It was very hard to get over the loss of Alison, but it gradually got easier with time, and I continued to find a great deal of joy in my role as a mother to Craig. Seeing him grow up and reach his milestones was a constant source of pleasure to me.

However, I still suffered with anxiety, and sometimes it was worse than others. In particular, there were days when I could not stop thinking about my grandfather's strange behaviour, especially in the final years of his life. I was still angry with him for taking his negative feelings towards my mother out on me. It was not fair to blame her for what had happened to Francis, and none of it was my fault. Even if Grandad had been beginning to show signs of dementia, or if it was a side-effect of his as yet undiagnosed cancer – either of which scenario is possible – it had all been very hard.

I tried to discuss Grandad's strange behaviour in his latter years with my aunts and uncles, thinking that now he was gone, perhaps we could talk calmly and rationally about him. This was a mistake on my part. He was their father, after all, and, while they had all had their ups and downs with him, nobody wanted to hear my story. It was hurtful for them to hear what I had to say about a man they remembered fondly as a hard-working father, who most people respected as a kind man and a gentleman. Grandad was all those things, and more, but he had also been my tormentor at a stage in my life when I was particularly vulnerable.

As a mother, I was also increasingly aware of the impact of sexual abuse on children, and I had to accept that the abuse that I had suffered as a little girl had had a big impact on my life. I sometimes panicked that Craig might be abused. It was hard for me to give permission for him to attend sleepovers with his little friends, even with people I knew and trusted. I was afraid that my excessive fears would hurt him when all I wanted was to give Craig a wonderful childhood. I just wanted support, but I was looking for it in the wrong place. I can see now that it was unfair of me to expect my family to be able to listen to my stories of abuse and to help me; nobody can be objective about a difficult situation involving an abusive member of their own family.

Eventually, I realised that I needed more support than my relatives, and even John, could offer me. I had heard of the Rape Crisis Centre, on Leeson Street in Dublin's city centre, so I rang them up and made an appointment to talk about the abuse I had suffered as a young child, how it had had a long-term impact on my emotional health, and how I had felt when Grandad came into my room at night.

I was nervous the first day I attended the Centre, but my counsellor – a lovely woman called Anne-Marie – was kind and patient, and she made me feel at ease. For three years, I attended therapy once a week. It sounds strange to say it, but I really looked forward to those sessions, which became the highlight of my week. I would even dress up a bit, do my hair, and make a day out of it; John would take care of Craig on the days that I went.

It felt wonderful to be able to talk to someone who did not judge me or tell me that I was lying and inventing my problems. One of the first things that Anne-Marie explained to me was that we all have our personal space. She stood up and extended her two arms, and then turned around in a circle. She explained that we all have the right to decide whether or not to invite someone else inside our personal space and that somebody who insists on penetrating another's personal space without permission is actually being abusive.

I realised then that a big problem for me growing up had been a complete lack of boundaries. I had never really understood that I was an autonomous person, a girl who was – or should have been – completely separate from everyone else. I had grown up viewing myself as little more than the bodily manifestation of my grandmother's grief, and the source of my grandfather's anger. For most of the people I met, I seemed to be a walking, living, breathing symbol of tragedy and not an ordinary little girl. I was the Stardust Baby, not just Lisa Lawlor. I had never really understood that I was my own person. I had not felt able to tell anyone when I was being abused, and only when I started looking after Craig did I begin to understand that I had the capacity and responsibility to create my own happiness.

Even after just a few sessions of therapy with Anne-Marie, I could feel my anxiety receding, and I knew that it was helping me to be a better person, and a better mother to my little boy. Gradually, over the three years I attended the Rape Crisis Centre, I gained a much greater understanding of myself, and started being able to see my family and our shared history more objectively.

Many things that had not been clear to me when I was growing up became obvious. My grandmother – Mam, who was my mother in all but name – was not just bereaved and grieving, but had become chronically depressed after the death of Francis. The younger of my aunts and uncles, who were themselves still children when Francis died, had been emotionally neglected, and they had all suffered psychological damage as a result. How could they not have? This was not Mam's fault, or Grandad's, or mine, but just a result of the circumstances. As teenagers, they were at a sensitive age in their psychological development when they lost their brother to the fire. Then, when they needed their mother more than ever before, Mam was not fully emotionally available to them, because she was dealing with her own devastation and with a very demanding baby. For most of them, the consequences were horrendous and had a negative impact on their whole lives. The Stardust hurt them, too.

I will never fully understand why Grandad behaved towards me the way he did when I was a teenager, but I learned in therapy that it was in no way my fault, and that his behaviour had contributed to the escalation of my anxiety. I learned to move on, too, from the sexual abuse that I had experienced as a child.

Steadily, I was becoming a much happier, more well-rounded person, and I knew it. I also knew that, while being a mother to Craig was a wonderful source of personal fulfilment for me, I craved the experience of biological motherhood, and for the first time I was sure that I deserved to have this dream come true. I wanted to get pregnant, to feel the baby growing and kicking inside me, to give birth and to raise my biological child alongside my son, Craig, my lovely boy.

My desire to become pregnant and give birth grew. I imagined how lovely it would be to have a family with John. I felt that I would miss Mam and my parents less if I was a mother myself, and that by not having a baby, I was failing to fulfil my destiny. I asked John for a child and told him that I thought we could be wonderful parents together.

The problem was that John already had four children – and feeling that he had completed his family, he had had a vasectomy long before I had even met him. The one thing that John could not do for me was give me a baby.

"There must be something we can do, John," I said. "Bear in mind that I am only in my twenties and you're in your early fifties. All of my friends will be having babies soon and I would love to be a mother at the same time as them."

"I'll see what I can do," said John.

John and I went to the hospital to see if he could have his vasectomy reversed, but he was advised against even trying; a reversal was unlikely to work, and there was no point in him going through a painful procedure that was not going to make any difference anyway. I cried all the way home, and back at the house I cut myself again for the first time in years. John was furious with me when he saw the marks a few days later.

"I know you're upset, Lisa," he said. "But this is not going to help. I never want to see you doing this again."

Then we had another idea – I had heard of sperm donation, and knew that this was available in Dublin for single women who wanted to have babies, or whose husbands or partners were infertile. Perhaps, I thought, this would be perfect for me. I discussed the idea with John, and he agreed that this could be a solution to our problem, and assured me that he would have no issues raising a child who was not biologically his. John said that love is what makes a family.

After consulting the telephone directory, John and I made an appointment at a clinic that offered exactly what we were looking for.

"Ah, Jesus, Lisa," said John as we drove towards the clinic. "Are we doing the right thing here? Are you sure you can cope with the stress of a new baby? I know we have Craig, but I'm talking about a new-born. A new-born baby is a very big commitment. You can't put the baby back in the cupboard when you're finished playing with it."

"I know all about babies," I said, a little stung that John was questioning my competence in this area when Craig was doing so well.

The doctor at the clinic, a young woman in a white lab coat, was very friendly. She sat us down and quickly explained how the system worked, offering to answer any questions we might have before I went through the procedure.

"There'll only be one baby, though, right?" John asked. "She's not going to have triplets or something?"

"Oh yes," the doctor said. "This is not like IVF. There's no bigger chance than average of having a multiple birth."

"That's good," said John. "I'm too old to have a football team of kids scurrying about the place."

"How do we know the sperm isn't, you know, from someone weird or…?" I asked. "Like, I want to make sure the baby is going to be healthy and normal. I mean, obviously I will love the baby no matter what, but how can I be sure we're giving it the best possible chance in life?"

"You've nothing to worry about there," she reassured me. "All our sperm comes from Denmark, and it's donated by healthy, intelligent young students who just want to help childless couples become parents. We're talking about top-quality genetic material."

"Well," John said. "That sounds good."

"Have you got a photograph of the donor?" I asked. "I'd love to see what my baby might look like, if it takes after the father."

The doctor smiled and shook her head.

"I'm afraid not," she said. "It's all done anonymously. But they screen all the donors very carefully, so you've absolutely nothing to worry about. They're all very clever, handsome young men, and you can be sure that your baby will be from good stock."

"Jesus," John muttered. "This reminds me of getting the cows artificially inseminated down on the farm."

"Okay then," I said. "Let's do it."

I got ready, removing the clothing from the lower half of my body, and climbed up on the surgical couch. The doctor draped a cloth over my hips and, instructing me to part my legs gently, used an object very like a turkey baster to insert the sperm. I closed my eyes, crossed my fingers, and prayed to my parents to help me in whatever way they could to make this baby happen.

The doctor kept chatting to me as she went through the procedure. I suppose she was trying to help me to relax and to take my mind off the absurdity of the whole situation.

"The Catholic church is still dead set against artificial insemination," she said conversationally. "They still don't approve of non-conventional forms of conception. We'd never have been allowed to do this in Ireland 20 years ago, but things have changed a lot around here. You'd be surprised how many women come in through our doors to use our services."

"I see," I said. "Well, I'm not very holy. I'm religious in my own way, but I don't go to church. I don't think God would mind how I get my baby – and it's not going to make any difference to the baby, is it?"

To my astonishment, the doctor then launched into a loud recitation of the Lord's Prayer over my prone body, while still doing her thing with the turkey baster.

"Just in case," she said. "A bit of prayer can't hurt, anyway!"

At this, John and I burst into near-hysterical laughter and took several minutes to calm down.

"Now," the doctor said as I got dressed. "Just take it very easy for the rest of the day. It'll improve your chances of conception if you keep your feet elevated. Don't have a bath or go swimming for the next three or four days and that will give the sperm the best possible chance to reach your egg and fertilise it."

I dangled my feet above my head all the way home in the car, trying to clench my body tight to hold the donor sperm in. I imagined it coursing through my body, looking for a nice, ripe egg to fertilise. I was very hopeful that, as I was still young, and as I wanted this baby so much, I was becoming pregnant right there and then.

"Lisa," John said. "I think you're taking the doctor too literally. Everyone is looking at us. I don't think you have to have your legs in the air *all* the time."

"I don't care who looks at us!" I said. "I want this to work and I'm going to do everything the doctor says."

As soon as we got home, I went to bed and carefully elevated my legs again. John went out, and when he came back hours later, I was still there, flicking through a magazine with my feet higher than my head.

"I think you can stand up now, Lisa," John said. "If that stuff hasn't reached an egg yet, it never will."

Unfortunately, my efforts to get pregnant with the donor sperm failed. My period came a couple of weeks later. I was devastated when I started to bleed and was forced to recognise that my dream had not come true as easily as I had hoped.

"I can't believe it, John," I cried. "I was sure that it was meant to be."

I went straight up to the graveyard in Sutton to tell my parents what had happened and to ask them for support. I prayed to them, begging them to intercede with God and help me to get pregnant the next time. I must have knelt beside their graves for hours. By the time I left the cemetery I felt a little better, as I was sure that my parents had heard me in my distress and would do what they could to intervene with God and help me to get the longed-for baby.

I tried to get pregnant over and over again with the donor sperm, for a fee of €800 each time. For whatever reason, it did not work; I suppose it just was not meant to be. Every time I got my period after each failed attempt, I went to the graveyard to ask my parents for help. Sometimes I sat beside their graves and just prayed quietly, and more than once I tried to hug my mother's grave by lying myself down on it and pressing my whole body against the cold ground, as though she might be able to feel the warm of my body through the soil. I had never felt as close to her there as I did to my father, and I suppose I thought that if I could get physically closer to her remains, I might feel more of a connection. I must have looked quite mad, but I was still convinced that Mum and Dad knew about my grief and my longing to give birth and that, somehow, they would be able to help.

Despite the fact that each attempt to get pregnant ended in bitter disappointment and tears, I never lost faith in my parents' ability to look down from heaven and help me in my hour of need. When I was a child, Mam had always taught me that my parents could hear me when I prayed. I knew that Mam had believed this herself, and she had never been anything but truthful with me, so I clung to this idea.

John was very good and paid uncomplainingly for every sperm donation until we reached number 10 or 11. By then, he was beginning to lose faith in the process and felt that we needed to take a different approach.

"This is a bit of a farce, Lisa," John said eventually. "I reckon you should be after having twins by now, if not triplets!"

Shortly after that, one of John's last cheques to the sperm donor clinic bounced and the doctor rang him to let him know that he would need to issue another one. For John, this was the last straw.

"When Lisa has a baby, I'll give you the money," John said to the doctor. "Is that all right? You've had an awful lot of money from us so far and there's no baby here to show for it. It seems to me you've got a great business model going – just tell people there's no guarantee, and they'll keep coming back to try again. It looks a lot like you're making a living off other people's desperation. How do we even know that the sperm is any good? It's come an awful long way; maybe it's gone off en route."

We gave up on the sperm donor clinic, and I tried to accept that I would never have a biological baby of my own to love. After all, I had Craig and I could not have loved him any more if he had grown inside my own body. I thought that life was dealing me another blow and that I would just get on with things, as I always did. But my desire for a baby grew and grew. By now, John was over 60, and had had a vasectomy over 20 years before. John, who had given me so much over the years, could not give me the baby I desired.

Although it was tough, I did my best to accept that I would never give birth. I had Craig, and I had John, and that was all I needed. I knew that I would never love any biological child more than I loved Craig. But sometimes fate intervenes. During a rocky patch in my relationship with John, I had a brief encounter with someone else. Shortly after that, I was staring at a positive pregnancy test that told me that a little baby was growing inside me.

It was not easy telling John about the pregnancy. Although it had not been my intention to get pregnant, I was so happy when I saw the positive test; all I wanted was for him to be as excited as I was. Understandably, however, he was quite shocked at first. After all, this meant that I had been with someone else.

"I'm sorry, John," I said. "I know that this wasn't part of your plan, and I didn't set out for this to happen, but now that I'm pregnant, I'm happy. I've always dreamed of having a baby, and I am so excited about this pregnancy, even if it's unplanned. I'll understand if you decide to walk away, but I hope that you will stay, because I love you as much as ever."

John did not have to think about it for long – he told me that, while he was not the baby's biological father, he would be the dad. After all, having no biological connection with Craig had not stopped either of us from being his loving parents. The funny thing was, John was about to become a grandfather at the same time, because both Jane and April, his daughters, were expecting too.

Despite how unconventional the situation was, my pregnancy was one of the happiest times in my life. It was so exciting seeing the changes happening to my body and knowing that, safe inside me, my little son or daughter was growing and developing. I registered for maternity care with the Rotunda Maternity Hospital and visited regularly for my appointments. John came with me to all my scans. He held my hand and we both looked excitedly at the screen when the technician showed us the baby's tiny heart, beating away inside me. The lady doing my scan assumed that John was my father.

"Isn't your dad very good," she said, "coming along with you for your scans?"

John and I just looked at one another and smiled. By this time, we were used to people's misunderstandings and they no longer upset us.

The hospital staff were all very kind – they knew that I had a history of anxiety, and they did their best to reassure me, including referring me to a psychiatrist who would be able to help me to manage my anxiety during the pregnancy.

The psychiatrist was a kind man called Doctor Sheehan. He was very patient with me; I blush now, when I think about how naïve I was. The first day I saw him, when I was about nine weeks pregnant, I announced to him that I was going to have a caesarean, because I did not feel like giving birth. Doctor Sheehan had to explain that I would only have a caesarean if it was medically indicated, and that as I was a healthy young woman, it probably would not be. He said that my body was designed by nature to go through pregnancy and birth and that there was no reason why it would not go well.

"What?" I said. "I've no choice but to go through labour? But I don't want to do that! Surely there must be a better way to get the baby out?"

"We have great staff here," Doctor Sheehan said. "They'll be with you every step of the way, and they will make sure that you have everything you need."

"But doctor," I said. "What if I break in half? How many women break in half when they're having a baby?"

Doctor Sheehan actually laughed a little at that.

"Would it surprise you to know that, in the history of the world, not one single woman has split in two giving birth?" he asked.

"All right," I said, unconvinced.

"Lisa," Doctor Sheehan said. "I know that you are worried, and having a baby can be a scary prospect. I'm not going to tell you that it is going to be easy, but I want you to know that you can have this baby, and when you are holding your little child in your arms, you will feel so proud of yourself for what you have achieved."

The pregnancy continued to go well. I had come off the medication I took for my anxiety, and I was able to manage without it. I returned to the Rape Crisis Centre for some additional support because I felt very vulnerable at the time. The support I received from my counsellor at the Rape Crisis Centre was invaluable. I remember telling Anne-Marie one day that I was scared about giving birth in the maternity hospital because I was sure that I would be lonely without Mam.

"I just think I'm going to feel so terribly alone," I told Anne-Marie.

Then, embarrassingly, I burst into tears.

"It just seems so unfair," I wailed. "Most women have their mothers there when they have a baby, but I won't, and I am going to have to experience everything all by myself."

Anne-Marie smiled, and spoke to me in her low reassuring voice.

"Lisa," she said "You won't be alone at all. You'll be there with your perfect little baby. You're going to be fine. Don't worry."

I was so excited when I reached all the milestones – the first kick, the first stranger in the supermarket congratulating me and wishing me well. I loved looking at myself in a full-length mirror and seeing how my body was changing as the baby grew inside me. I had a mould made of my belly to hang on the wall so that I would never forget what my blooming body looked like.

Then, when I was eight months along, John fainted one day. I called for an ambulance, and he was rushed off to hospital. I went with him in the ambulance and begged the doctors to do what they could. John was diagnosed with a heart complaint and had surgery to install a pacemaker. The cardiologist reassured us that he would be fine, and would soon make a full recovery. A few days after John came home, he suddenly felt unwell during dinner and was rushed off to hospital again. He was diagnosed with atrial fibrillation, which is an irregular heartbeat. Since then, John has had to take beta blockers. Of course, I was worried by John's illness, especially as it had started during my pregnancy, but we both did our best to remain positive and focused on the future.

The pregnancy went so well, I was surprised by the maelstrom of emotions I felt when I went to the hospital and was induced – the baby was two weeks overdue. As soon as the very first labour pains kicked in, I started to think about how I was about to give birth for the first time, and would have no mother to show my baby to, or ask for advice. I cried all evening.

"I'll give you something to help you to calm down," the midwife said, and gave me diazepam. That took the edge off my agitation for a while, but when the pains got stronger, I started to get even more upset. Then they injected me with pethidine, telling me that I would be completely functional and would even be able to get up and go for little walks, despite the medication. Just a few minutes after the injection, I went to the bathroom, and when I was leaving, I walked straight into the wall.

I was in labour for 54 hours altogether – 30 hours of slow labour at the beginning, and then 24 hours of active labour. There were times when I was convinced that I was dying, and prayed aloud to my mother for help. Poor John, who was still recovering from heart surgery, was with me every step of the way; he was given a sleeping mat on the floor so that he could lie down and try to get some rest, but I felt that I needed him and kept waking the poor man up.

The midwives tried to help me in all sorts of ways, and eventually it was time for the epidural. I was so excited and pleased to see the anaesthetist, I tried to hug him. The labour continued, but the pain was more bearable now.

As I entered my 55th hour of labour, John sat up.

"Jesus, Lisa," he said. "I don't feel very well. It's the atrial fibrillation again."

I decided that as John had been there for me this whole time, perhaps he needed me there for him. I gathered my forces and with one final push, my beautiful daughter came into the world. She was a big, healthy baby and she opened her little mouth and roared as John held her in his arms and looked down at her.

"Well," said John. "I feel a hell of a lot better now."

John has never had atrial fibrillation since.

I had been badly torn in labour, but in the first minutes after the baby came into the world, I did not care about anything but her. Someone came and sewed me up, but I only had eyes for my precious child. Doctor Sheehan was right – I was so proud of myself for having gone through labour, and for having given life to this beautiful baby.

"Her name is Matilda," I said, gazing down at the baby's slate-blue eyes as she lay cradled in my arms.

"It certainly is not!" said John. "That's a horrible name! If you call her that, you'll give me another heart attack!"

We discussed various options for the baby's name, and John suggested that I call her Frances, after my father. She is Frances on her baptismal and her birth certificate, but we have called her "Frankie" from the start, because I didn't want her to feel burdened by the awful story of Francis's death.

Because John had experienced some heart symptoms while I was giving birth, he was advised to pop into the Mater Hospital for a quick check-up. He knew the cardiologist from previous appointments, but she was unaware that John was about to become a father again and got quite a shock when he told her that I had just had a baby.

"Goodness, John," the doctor said. "I thought you were past all that."

"Believe me," said John. "I thought so too."

The day after giving birth, I brought Frankie home. About two or three days afterwards, I found myself becoming completely overwhelmed with emotion. I started to wonder if I was capable of being a mother to this little baby at all. I started to worry that at some point she might be sexually abused, as I had been. I assumed that I was having problems because of my anxiety, or because of the way I had been brought up, or both. I made an appointment to see the psychiatrist at the maternity hospital. Doctor Sheehan was very kind and listened carefully to all of my concerns. I explained that I was feeling lonely and incompetent, and that I was doubting my own abilities.

"I don't want you to worry about this too much, Lisa," Doctor Sheehan said. "Having a new baby is a lot to adjust to, and it is perfectly normal to feel a little overwhelmed at times. What you are describing is not at all unusual. You're going to be fine."

It was such a relief to learn that many women experience similar issues, and that it is completely normal. I was so used to thinking of myself as damaged and broken, it never occurred to me that there might be plenty of women who felt the same way.

Craig was seven when Frankie was born, and at first his nose was quite of joint about having a baby sister. He complained about all the noise she made, and I knew that he was anxious about being displaced in my affections, and worried that I would feel differently about him now that I had a baby of my own. Soon, however, he got used to having a baby around, and he was a wonderful big brother. I showed Craig that there is plenty of love in the family to go around, and he soon understood that he was no less precious to me just because we do not share any DNA.

Frankie's christening was a happy day, although I wished that my parents could have known about the new baby, and hoped that they were looking down from heaven at us. We asked two of John's children to be her godparents, and had a small celebration back at the house afterwards.

Although John had expressed understandable misgivings about the baby when I told him that I was pregnant, now that Frankie was here, he was so excited to be a dad again, and he was very good at it. We bought a pram for Frankie, but I hardly ever had to use it, because John carried her everywhere. He was also the proud grandfather of two beautiful little babies before the year was out; it was lovely for all three of them to have the opportunity to grow up together. Jane, April and I often met up and shared our experiences over a cup of coffee, talking for hours about all of the babies' little achievements.

John was so accepting of my decision to continue with my pregnancy and bring Frankie into the world, that I was hopeful he would also be accepting of my second pregnancy, which was confirmed when Frankie was four years old. As soon as I saw the positive test, I rang Liz, my best friend.

"I'm worried about how John will take it," I fretted. "I know I demanded a lot of him the last time. I don't think he's going to be impressed."

"I'm sure it'll be fine," Liz said. "John loves you, Craig and Frankie. I'm sure he'll welcome another baby into the family. He's such a wonderful father."

"Yeah," I said. "I hope so, because it was a surprise."

This time, however, it was not fine. John was furious that I had been unfaithful for a second time, and that I had been careless and become pregnant. He was in his mid-sixties then, and felt that he did not want to be the father of a small baby all over again, especially as a result of my infidelity. He told me that it was unfair of me to expect him to go through with it and that I had been very selfish.

"But John," I said. "I know you can be a great father to this baby, just like you are to Frankie and Craig."

I know now that I had been taking John, and his infinite patience, for granted for years. I had been thinking only of myself, and now I had broken John's trust in me.

"Not this time," John said. "I've had enough, and it's time you learned how to stand on your own two feet. You're on your own. I know that you've had a tough life, Lisa, but it's finally time you grew up. You're rearing this baby on your own, and I think for the first time you're going to realise the consequences of your actions."

John was right. All my life, first my grandmother and then my teachers had excused my failures and shortcomings on the basis that I was badly damaged because of the awful way in which I had lost my parents. I had picked up the message that I could excuse myself for anything, because of my tragic past.

Now, as a woman in my thirties, I had to learn the opposite: that no matter how awful the things that had happened to me were, I could not go through life blaming other people and difficult circumstances for all of my own problems. At some point, I was going to have to accept responsibility for myself and my own decisions.

After supporting me through so many ups and downs over almost 20 years, John felt that my second infidelity was such a breach of trust that he was justified in leaving me. Just like that, our relationship as intimate partners came to an end. I could hardly believe it. I was used to leaning on John and relying on him to sort out all my problems. At the same time, I didn't really blame him. I knew that I was being unfair to him, and that he was right in saying that I had pushed him too far. I was desperately upset, but I accepted his decision.

My feelings at this time were complicated and overwhelming. I knew that I could not be angry with John, because in truth I had betrayed his trust, but at the same time, I mourned for all that I had thrown away, and felt bereft, as though I had lost a father and a partner at the same time. It seemed as though my life was over.

My best friend, Liz, was a huge support to me. Whenever I felt that I couldn't cope, I turned to her, and she assured me that I was a good mother and that I would be fine. My friend and neighbour, Lindsay, was also there for me, reassuring me that everything was going to work out. Little by little, I became more confident in my abilities to take care of myself and my children. As John said, it was time that I learned how to stand on my own two feet.

Towards the end of the pregnancy, I woke up one day feeling unwell. Convinced that I was having the baby, I went into the hospital, where I talked to a nurse at admission.

"I'm pretty sure I'm in labour," I told the woman. "I'd like to be admitted to the hospital."

"Not a bit of it," she said. "Look at you – you're still able to talk. You're fine. It's just your imagination. You can go on home, because when you're actually in labour, you'll know all about it."

I went home that night and went to bed early. At three in the morning, I woke up in horrendous pain, and went straight to summon Lindsay, who lived a few doors away. I remember holding onto the counter in the kitchen, my knuckles actually white. I was in much more pain than I had been with Frankie. I remembered a time many years before when a friend, Kim, had gone into labour in front of me. She had been in too much pain to get into the car, and I had panicked that we would not make it to the hospital in time. Now I knew how Kim had been feeling.

Lindsay's face was as white as a sheet, and she looked terrified.

"Jesus, Lisa, you don't look all right," Lindsay said. "What should I do?"

"I'm having this baby, Lindsay," I said. "I've been through this before, and I know exactly what's happening."

"Jesus," Lindsay said. "Will I ring an ambulance for you? What's the best thing right now?"

"No," I said. "Calm down. I'll drive myself there."

I asked Lindsay to stay with the children, took the car keys, and started driving myself to hospital. Every single traffic light that I encountered seemed to be red. At one point, I was not sure that I would even make it to the hospital on time. I pulled the car in at the side of the road, near a pedestrian crossing. Suddenly I was creased with pain. I took a few deep breaths, and wondered if I had made a terrible mistake in deciding to drive myself. Maybe I needed help. I rolled the window down and stuck out my head.

"Hey you!" I shouted at a man crossing the road. "I'm having a baby here!"

"You're what?" the man shouted back.

The man blinked at me and stopped in the middle of the road. I realised that he was drunk. He just stared at me for a minute and then ambled on, laughing to himself.

"Well, shit," I said. "I'm just going to have to handle this myself. I'll just have to cross my legs until I get to the hospital."

I turned the key in the ignition and drove on as quickly as I could, doing my best to ignore the periodic pains I was experiencing. When I arrived at the hospital, I pulled into the disabled parking space in front of the main entrance, and waddled in to get some help.

"I'm having a baby!" I said to the nurse at the admission desk. "Help me!"

The nurse just looked at me with a bored expression.

"Are you sure?" she said. "If you just managed to drive here, it's very unlikely. But as you're here anyway, we'll take a look."

When the nurse examined me, she announced that I was actually seven centimetres dilated, had clearly been in labour for some time, and that it would not be long before the baby was born.

"Get me an epidural while there's still time!" I shouted. "I'm not going through this without some medication!"

Meanwhile, Lindsay had called my Auntie Mary, who had got out of bed and come to the hospital to support me. The labour progressed quickly. I needed an episiotomy and a ventouse delivery, and had to have a lot of stitches, but my baby boy was big, beautiful and healthy, and that was really all I cared about.

After spending some time with me, Auntie Mary left to go home. My cousin Mary replaced her, telling me that everything was going to be okay, and providing me with reassurance and support. After Mary had left, I was on my own with my little son. I picked him up and looked at his precious, tiny features and his little fists. I was so happy that he was fine, but I did feel desperately lonely. I rang Liz and told her about the baby. She congratulated me and promised to visit as soon as she could. That made me feel a little better, at least for a minute.

"Hello there," said one of the midwives, poking her head around the curtain and looking in at me. "How are you managing? Are you on your own? Where's the baby's dad?"

I felt ashamed and embarrassed about not having anyone with me, so I lied to her.

"Oh," I said. "He's in the army and he couldn't make it, but they'll be giving him leave soon enough and I won't be on my own for long."

"Have you no family that can help you? It's tough to be alone at a time like this."

"My Auntie Mary and my cousin were just here," I said. "My mum and dad died in the Stardust."

I was very upset and close to tears, but I did my best not to show any emotion. I was terrified that, if I did, the hospital staff would decide that I was mentally unstable and would try to take the baby away. I was worried that the great anxiety I had felt, and displayed, during labour was enough to make anyone think that I was an incapable person. I remained as calm as I could during my stay in hospital, all alone as I was on the maternity ward, while the other women proudly showed their babies to their visitors.

The next day, the doctor came round, checked my stitches, and told me that I was ready to go home. It was hard to believe, because I felt as though I had been hit by a bus, and the emotional pain was as draining as the physical. I rang Lindsay and asked her to pass the phone to Craig. I told Craig that I was on my way home with his baby brother, and got out of bed to pack my bags. I looked high and low for my car keys, but they were nowhere to be seen. Eventually, I gave up looking for them. On my own, I staggered down the hospital corridor with my legs spread wide because my episiotomy stitches hurt so much, and into the elevator with the baby in one hand and my bags in the other.

When I reached the lobby, Craig, Frankie and John were all there to collect me. I could hardly believe it. The last time I had seen John, he was still so angry with me.

"John!" I said. "You came!"

"Well, I promised your grandmother I'd always be there for you, and I'm a man who keeps his promises," John said. "Did you think I would let you bring that baby home on your own?"

"Can I see the baby, Mammy?" squeaked little Frankie, who was very excited about having a new little baby brother.

When I bent down to show the baby to Frankie, I saw that Craig and John had dressed her in Spiderman pyjamas that were too small for her, and that they had put her shoes on the wrong feet. I immediately panicked, thinking that someone might see her and laugh at me, because I always kept her dressed so well.

"Get her into the car before someone sees her!" I said. "The absolute state of her!"

"Calm the fuck down," said John, laughing. "She's grand. We're just here to pick up you and the baby. Nobody cares what Frankie is wearing."

I took a few deep breaths and recognised the sense in what John was saying.

"I've lost my car keys," I said to John. "I've no idea where they are."

John and I went outside to see if the car had been towed, as by now it had been in a disabled parking bay for 48 hours. Amazingly, not only was the car still there, but it was unlocked, and the keys were still in the ignition. John helped me to install the baby in his little baby seat, and I got into the car − crying out as I sat down because I was in so much pain − and drove home with my family. I was so grateful that, although he was rightfully angry with me, John had once again turned up and saved the day.

John was a great friend to me at this time in my life, as he had always been, but he was determined not to become a father figure to baby Lennon (as I called him); he was understandably upset that I had been unfaithful to him again. I knew that he was right, so I did not push it, even though I was very upset when he said he didn't want to come to the christening. Fortunately, I had a lot of support from my friends Lindsay and Liz, my cousin Mary, and my Auntie Carol. Even though Craig was just a young boy, he did everything he could to help.

Once again, as when Frankie was born, I could not stop thinking about my mother, and wishing that she were there for me. I hoped that, somehow, she knew about the baby and wished me well. From a very early age, Lennon suffered from eczema, asthma and allergies, and needed a lot of care. I stayed up with him on many nights, rocking him and praying to my parents that he would be all right.

At first, John made a point of keeping his distance from Lennon, but gradually, he could not help bonding with him, and by the time Lennon turned two, John doted on him, as he had doted on Frankie. Since then, John and I have been best friends and co-parents, but we have decided to remain apart. Although I do have regrets about how I treated John, and huge gratitude to him for his endless kindness, I have never regretted becoming a mother.

The first big step towards my personal healing was the day when I knew that Craig was coming home with me and that I was going to be his mammy. The second was the day I realised that I needed professional help and started attending the Rape Crisis Centre. The third was realising that I needed to experience pregnancy and biological motherhood, and having Frankie and Lennon. My three children have given me the chance to lead a new and better life.

13

Beyond the Stardust

One night in 2018, I was in a pub in the north inner city – the Seventy-Four Talbot on Talbot Street – when a girl I knew from the Sheriff Street area where I had grown up, Nicola, recognised me.

"Lisa Lawlor!" she said. "Come here to me. You're wanted downstairs."

"What are you talking about?" I asked. "Who wants me?"

"Quick!" she said. "Come downstairs with me for a second. It'll all be clear then."

Nicola took me by the arm and led me downstairs.

"What's going on?" I asked.

As soon as I got downstairs, I saw several of the key members of the Stardust Campaign seated at the bar: Antoinette and Chrissie Keegan, who had been fighting for justice for the Stardust families for 38 years – since they lost their two beautiful girls to the fire – and several others. The group had been campaigning that evening, and they were all wearing special campaign T-shirts.

Antoinette rose up when she saw me, and I started to cry. I had not seen her in years, but I would have recognised her anywhere.

"Lisa," said Antoinette. "You're very welcome. Will you join us for a drink?"

I hugged Chrissie and Antoinette, and Antoinette handed me one of the campaign T-shirts.

"Put that on if you like," she said. "You're one of us. You always have been. It's nice to see you looking so well."

I had left the Stardust Campaign 18 years earlier, after attending just a few meetings and doing very little, because I was not strong enough for it. At the time, I had been too insecure, too emotionally unwell and too fragile to be of any use. I had felt so guilty about it ever since, wondering if I should have stayed and made a bigger effort, that I had actually avoided Antoinette and Chrissie and the whole campaign, afraid that I had let them down and that they might be angry with me. It was such a relief to find them as kind and open as always, and extremely welcoming to me after all these years.

Antoinette explained that the campaign was still working hard to secure justice for the Stardust families, and she asked me if I would like to get involved again. Now, as a mature woman with three children of her own, I knew that I had so much more to offer than before, and that I was in a much better place than I had been as a younger woman. I did not hesitate, and told

Antoinette that I would do whatever I could, and that I was grateful to her for all that she had done in the intervening years.

I rang Antoinette the next day, and she invited me to her house. I dropped over that night. We sat over a cup of tea and Antoinette explained what the campaign had been doing. Their latest thing was to have 48,000 postcards – a thousand postcards for each victim of the fire – signed and delivered to the Irish Attorney General in support of a new inquest. They were on the campaign trail almost every day, bringing their message to the people of Dublin outside supermarkets and shopping centres all over the country and getting people to sign their postcards. They were determined not to let their message die. The fact that so many of the parents of the victims had already passed away did not dissuade them at all – if anything, it made them even more determined to make sure that justice was done before they were all gone. I was humbled by all the hard work they had been doing for years, while also living with their terrible grief. It had been as much as I could manage just to keep going, so I could not even imagine where they found the courage and strength to go on.

I joined Antoinette and the others on the campaign trail a few times and was amazed by their dedication and all the work they had been doing. For the most part, the people we met were interested in and curious about the campaign, and generally very supportive of it.

"And who are you?" a few people asked me – Antoinette and Chrissie had been on television so often that most people knew who they were, but I had not been in the media for years.

"I was orphaned by the Stardust," I told them. "Both my parents were killed in the fire."

Even after so many years, most Dublin north-siders over a certain age still knew who I was once I told them about my parents.

"Oh my God," I heard, over and over again. "Are you Lisa? The Stardust Baby? God, love, I bet you have a book in you. Have you ever considered writing one?"

More than one elderly person crossed themselves when I confirmed that I was indeed the Stardust Baby.

"God love you, pet," they said. "I used to pray for you when you were little. I saw you in the paper so many times. I've often wondered how you were getting on."

Everyone was very kind and said that they had seen me in the papers or on the television many times when I was a little girl, and that they hoped I had had a nice life. A lot of them asked me questions about who had brought me up, and whether I had suffered. I was strong enough to answer their questions without getting upset.

On 25 September 2019, the Irish Attorney General, Séamus Woulfe, finally granted the Stardust Campaign the second inquest that they had been fighting to achieve for decades, stating that it was in their interest, and in the interest of justice, and that the deaths had not been investigated adequately at the time. Antoinette rang me to let me know that a press conference had been organised, and that I was to be one of the main speakers. Even after all these years, the

Stardust Baby was still enough of a draw for the media to be interested in the story.

"Oh God, Antoinette," I said. "I don't know about that. I'd be mortified in front of the reporters."

"Well, I'm counting on you, Lisa," said Antoinette. "We're all counting on you. I just know that your words can make a big difference."

As the day of the press conference approached, I got more and more nervous. I was sure that I would do or say something wrong and did not want to let Antoinette and Chrissie down after all their hard work. On the day of the conference, I rang John in a panic and told him that I was not going to go because I didn't think I could cope with all the attention. John helped me to calm down.

"It's only going to be an hour or two, Lisa," John said. "I know that you can do it."

The press conference was to be held at Buswell's Hotel, which is a Dublin institution, directly opposite the government buildings on Kildare Street. It is where all the politicians go for a drink after work.

On the day of the conference, I dressed in formal clothing, mindful of how Mam had always made sure that I was well-dressed for media events as a child, so that I would reflect well on the family. Although I do not usually wear glasses, I did on this occasion, because I felt that along with a hat, they offered me some protection from the prying eyes of the media. They were something for me to hide behind.

I recognised the names and faces of some of the media people who came to the conference. The well-known *Irish Times* journalist Kitty Holland was a friendly face. The reporters from RTE television, the national broadcaster, were pleasant and matter of fact, telling us where to stand and how to move for the television cameras. I said everything that I had come to say: that the Stardust victims and their families had been treated shamefully by the government of the day, and every government subsequently; that the survivors and their loved ones had lived for years in the shadow of the fire, their grief compounded by the way they were treated by the authorities, and that the story of the Stardust could not be said to be over until justice had been done.

That night, the children and I watched the press conference together on the television. Frankie and Lennon took turns trying on my glasses and saying, "Hello, this is Lisa from the Stardust." Even now, they occasionally beg me to put my glasses on and do "the Stardust voice".

"You were great, Mam," said Craig. "I'm proud of you."

John had advised me to go ahead with the press conference because he felt that it was the right thing to do, and because he felt that it would be good for me. He was correct on both counts. When it was over, I felt a huge sense of relief, and I also felt very proud of myself. It had taken a lot of work to get my anxiety levels sufficiently under control to be able to face the rows of cameras and reporters, but I had done it. I know that I would never have been able to if my children and John had not helped me to become the stronger woman I am today.

Although it took me some time to recognise his wisdom, today I am very grateful to John for leaving me when I had finally pushed him too far, and for forcing me to accept that it was time for me to grow up and take responsibility for myself. When John told me that our relationship was over, and that he was moving out, I was absolutely devastated at first. My best friend, Liz, could tell you many stories about the countless hours I spent crying about how my life was over, and how I would never be able to manage without John, who had been doing everything for me since I was 18 years old.

The reality is, that at 35, I was still failing to take responsibility for myself and my decisions, because I assumed that, no matter what I did, John would always be there to pick up the pieces and deal with my mistakes. All my childhood, I had been taught that I was so broken I would never amount to much. I had never queried this assessment of myself, and instead of learning to become more assertive and resilient in adulthood, I had seen John as not just my lover and partner, but also my protector and even my parent. In this way, I had remained suspended in a sort of permanent psychological childhood – the Stardust Baby, whose life had been destroyed before she even learned how to talk.

When he left me, John forced me to take a cold, hard look at myself. I could see how I had allowed myself to stay weak – and now I could also see how I had already become stronger, more resilient and more resourceful in my role as a mother to Craig, Frankie, and Lennon. While I knew that John would always be my supporter, and the children's beloved dad, I learned to accept that I *am* able to take care of myself. I am damaged, but not broken. I am bereaved, but life goes on. As the song goes, I get knocked down, but I get up again.

Being a mother allowed me to start moving on from the awfulness of the Stardust fire and the chaos that I grew up in and that trailed along behind me as I entered adulthood. I often tell people that if I had not become a mother when Craig came into my life, I would not be alive today. I mean that completely literally. As this book was nearing completion, Craig came to me with a note that he had written, asking if I could find a place to squeeze it in. He thanked me for coming into his life when I did and said that his love for me, his mam, is immeasurable. I have tried to explain to Craig that he has given me so much more than I have ever given him. He will never know the extent to which he saved me.

As a woman who has been blessed with three wonderful children, I know that my most important job is to ensure that they have happy childhoods and the opportunity to follow their dreams without being plagued by self-doubt. All I have ever wanted is for them to feel absolutely loved and to have a strong foundation on which to build their lives. I know that my children will face challenges, as we all must do, but I am confident that John and I have given them a solid foundation that will help them to succeed in whatever they choose to do. I have learned how to take care of them without panicking, although we did all get a terrible fright when Lennon had a serious allergic reaction to shellfish and had to be rushed to hospital (for those who live with anxiety, when something awful really does happen, it can seem like a confirmation of their worst fears).

When I look at my three perfect children, I feel a sense of love for them that is almost fierce and even a little frightening sometimes. When I think about something bad happening to them, I feel that I can understand the determination that made my father go back into the blazing Stardust disco to retrieve his beloved Maureen, even though he must have known that it was likely he would not make it out alive. I can forgive my father for doing what he did, even though the result was that I would grow up with no parents at all.

While my own childhood had its bright moments, I still live with difficult memories of some of the terrible things I experienced. I know that if anyone treated my children the way some people treated me, I would do whatever it took to make them stop. Like Francis, I would go into a blazing building, if I had to.

John has continued to be a wonderful father to Craig, Frankie, and Lennon. They see him every day, and we make all the big parenting decisions together. I know that he will never let me down. Since John and I split up, I have had a couple of relationships with other men. It was hard for them both to accept the big part that John will always play in my life and in that of my children, so neither relationship lasted. John has a key to my door, and he will always have one. So far as I am concerned, he is Craig, Frankie, and Lennon's dad, and has every right to come in and out of their home without knocking. We have always worked together to provide a loving environment for our children, and ensuring that this will continue to be the case is my number one priority. Maybe one day I will meet a kind man who is prepared to accept John's presence in our lives, but if I never do, that's also okay.

The wonderful young man that Craig has become has confirmed to me that John and I have done a good job as his parents. When Craig was still in school, his teachers always told me that he was an exceptionally sweet-natured child, with a real creative streak. They all said that he was perfectly happy so long as he had some crayons or coloured pencils and paper to express himself with. By the time Craig reached his mid-teens, he already knew what he wanted to do.

"Mam," said Craig. "I've made up my mind. I'm going to be a hairdresser."

I could only laugh, because when Craig was little, he came to the hairdresser with me all the time. From early childhood, he has loved fashion and making a dramatic appearance. He is like me in that way. John had always joked that if I kept taking Craig with me to the hairdresser, he would think the salon was his real home. It turns out that John was right – again. To nobody's surprise, as soon as he started his hairdressing apprenticeship, Craig took to the work like a duck to water. I am sure that he is going to have a wonderful career. Hopefully, he will help this proud mammy keep her hair in perfect condition.

Making a fuss of the children at important milestones, such as birthdays, and Holy Communions, is important to me. Because these events can be bittersweet for me, I only invite a few very close friends and relatives rather than throwing a big party. I always miss my parents terribly on those occasions, and I know that the stress of having to take care of a big crowd would be too much for me. The last thing I want to do is turn a happy day sad by weeping for hours. I remember how hard it was for Mam at my Holy Communion, and how traumatic it was for me to see her weeping all day long. I do cry sometimes, wishing that my parents were here to see my beautiful children growing up, but I take care to do it discreetly.

Something else that really matters to me is being truthful and honest with my children. They have all asked why I do not have a mammy and a daddy, because most of their friends have grandparents. I explain that my parents died long ago in a fire, and that in part because of what happened that night, the authorities in Ireland are much more careful today than they were then, which means that our country is safer now than before.

"Somebody was playing with matches," little Lennon said, very seriously, the first time he really understood what I was telling him. "And that's why *I'm* not allowed to have matches."

Lennon is a little rascal who would absolutely love to play with matches, so I like to think that my parents are somehow helping me to keep him safe.

I wish that I were on better terms with my extended family, but I have learned to accept that some of us are better off going our separate ways, because when we get together, we only end up hurting each other. I have fond memories of many of my relatives: especially of Edel, Denis, and Alison, who were so kind to me when I was a child; of my cousin Evelyne, and of my cousin Mary, who has gone on to have a wonderful life and a fantastic job. Mary always was a high achiever. I am in constant contact with Alison's daughter Emma, who is now a fantastic young woman with a beautiful baby of her own. I am glad to have had the opportunity to build a close friendship with my Lawlor cousins, Carla and Sharon. Unfortunately, so far as many of my relatives are concerned, I think it is better for us all for me to wish them well from a distance. The last thing I want to do is hurt them. None of us had it easy, and I am sure that we are all just doing our best.

For years, I have worked very hard to take care of my emotional health. I check in with a therapist every seven or eight months, and while I have not returned to the Rape Crisis Centre for a long time, I know that I can contact them in the future if I ever need to. I know that it is important not just for me, but for everyone, to invest in their mental and emotional health. I have learned to see the efforts I take to maintain my emotional health as a journey that I will always be on, because no matter what happens, life will always have its ups and downs.

I have found a path to happiness through my children, and my heart is filled with love for them – but there is still a little, yearning space that is always empty. It is the space where my parents, and the memories of the happy childhood I did not have, should be. I hope that one day I will be able to say a real goodbye to my parents in my heart.

I always had a strange feeling of emptiness when I stood by my mother's grave. After the fire, many of the victims were unrecognisable, and the powers that be wanted to get them all in the ground as quickly as possible. 40 years have passed since then. The surviving parents of the victims are getting older, and some of them are no longer with us. But so many unanswered questions about why the disaster happened, and why it was as terrible as it was, remain. Some of the families of the victims, including me, do not even know for sure if they are mourning at the right graves. Hopefully, that will not always be the case and one day we will be provided with some clarity.

When I was a child, my grandmother taught me that not just God, but also my parents, could hear my prayers. I realise that it sounds naïve, but I still believe this literally. I believe that my parents have been watching over me all my life and that, while I have certainly made some bad decisions in my time, they have helped me to make the right ones at the times when it really mattered. I see their intervention in all the great milestones of my life: meeting John; becoming a mother to Craig; giving birth to my two younger children. I believe that they helped me to make the decision to write this book and to share our story with the world.

In my parents' honour, and in memory of my beloved Mam, I have taught my children how to pray. Sometimes the little ones and I get into bed together and say the same old words that I was taught when I was a little girl: "Now I lay me down to sleep." They know that nothing bad can happen to them so long as I am here to care for them – and I know that it is my responsibility to keep not just them, but also myself, safe and well so that I always will be.

For me, prayer, therapy and caring for my children and helping them to prepare for the future is all about hope. Without hope, there is nothing. Learning to feel a sense of hope is what saved me from the heroin that blighted the lives of so many of my family members. Hope is what propelled me out of my childhood home and into the arms of the kind man who helped me to turn my life around. Hope is what made it possible for me to see myself as a mother and a strong woman, rather than a frightened and broken little girl. Hope is what made me decide, as I approached the 40th anniversary of my parents' terrible death, that it was time to write this book.

The world is filled with terrible, tragic stories. It is filled with bereaved children. Many of these children will have been told, as I was, that they are broken and may never completely recover from the awful loss that they have suffered. My journey from bereavement to happiness was a long and circuitous one, and I learned a lot along the way. Most of all, I learned that, with hope, anyone can learn to be a better, stronger version of themselves.

Today, looking towards the second half of my life, I am very hopeful that it will be filled with joy, and also that – after all these years – the victims of the Stardust will finally get the justice they deserve.

Acknowledgements

As always, my love and heartfelt thanks to John, who has always been there for me, and who is a wonderful father and the best friend anyone could have. John, this book would not have happened without you. Thanks also to my fantastic children – Craig, Frankie and Lennon, and my lovely niece Emma, who is like a daughter to me – they were all with me through the lockdown of 2020 while I worked on this book and I love all four with all my heart. Craig and Emma, who are adults and old enough to understand what I am doing and why, have been supportive every step of the way. Thanks also to my close friends, Liz, Sandra, and Amanda. For years, I told them all that one day I would write a book, and they encouraged me to start.

I would like to thank my editor at Mirror Books, Jo Sollis, for taking on my book and for her kindness and support during the editing process. Her professional and personal care and attention to detail have been extraordinary.

Finally, thanks to Deirdre Nuttall, who helped me to get my story out of my head and onto the page and who made this adventure possible